Contents

A LARGE, OPEN AREA SITS IN THE HEART OF MODERN-DAY ROME. STARK WHITE COLUMNS rise here and there, some standing alone and others grouped in twos or threes. The stone foundations of once-glorious buildings peek through weeds. This site is the **Forum**, the center of social and political life in ancient Rome.

That Rome, and the people who lived in it, are gone. But their contributions to government, architecture, culture, and literature continue to influence and inspire cultures throughout the world.

The Origins of Rome and the Rise of Roman Culture

The official history of Rome begins in 753 B.C., when myth says Rome was founded by the legendary Romulus. But archaeological evidence shows that Rome began between 2000 and 1000 B.C., when Indo-Europeans migrated into what are now Italian lands and surrounding areas. One group, the Latins, built their settlements along some of the hills in the Tiber River valley. Below the hills, they established a common meeting place where they could gather at an easily fordable place along the Tiber. The area eventually became the Forum, around which the city of Rome grew.

A nearby cultural group, the Etruscans, were stronger and more advanced than the Latins. Some scholars believe that the Etruscans conquered the Latins in 625 B.C. Others argue that the Latins were influenced, but not overwhelmed, by the Etruscan culture. It is known that some early Roman kings were Etruscans. Between 625 and 509, Rome grew into an important city. In 509 B.C. the last Etruscan king was expelled from Rome. The people abolished the monarchy and established the Roman Republic, in which the state was governed by representatives of the people.

The Republic, which lasted from 509 B.C. until about 27 B.C., is considered one of Rome's most glorious periods. During this time, Rome became the dominant power in the civilized world. The Republic was replaced by the Empire when the first emperor of Rome, Octavian, was given the title of Augustus in 27 B.C. By then, there were very few places left in the known world that had not been touched in some way by Roman civilization.

During four hundred years of imperial rule, Rome began to weaken through a gradual breakdown of the government. By A.D. 476, the once-powerful Rome was in decline. For the next two hundred years, Rome was ruled by a number of German-born kings. Finally, in the sixth century, barbarian armies from northern Europe invaded Italy and took control of much of the country, including Rome.

For the next eight hundred years, Rome languished. The once-grand structures fell into ruin, and some were eventually buried. Thousands of records and writings by Roman historians, philosophers, and rulers were lost or forgotten. The Forum disappeared beneath rubble.

During the 1300s, a new historical period called the Renaissance began in Italy. During this era, there was a renewed interest in the ancient world. Scholars searched for old writings, explored the ruins, and observed what was left of art and architecture. Today, archaeologists study ruins and artifacts to understand how the Romans lived. Scholars pore over ancient texts and marvel at the wit and intelligence of Roman writers. Modern historians use the texts of Roman historians to piece together the story of the Roman culture. Artists study Rome's art and architecture to learn about their beauty.

It is important to study and learn from past cultures for a variety of reasons. The history of Roman civilization is part of the history of all world cultures. Studying how and why Rome rose, became powerful, and eventually disappeared allows modern scholars to discover how and why societies flourish and the problems that can lead to their downfall. Understanding the problems of a major civilization such as Rome can enable people today to learn from the experiences of the ancients.

Archaeologists work at Vindolanda, the site of an old Roman fort in northern England. By A.D. 180, the Romans had expanded their territory into what is now known as Great Britain.

Chapter I

THE RULERS OF ROME

Rome was one of the world's most magnificent cities for approximately five hundred years. Throughout that time, its culture and government grew and changed to meet the demands of the Roman people.

Historians divide Roman history into three sections, based on the type of leadership the civilization had at the time. Kings shaped the path of early Rome. A long series of consuls maintained order and stability during the Roman Republic. The dictatorial powers of the Roman emperors during the later part of Rome's history eventually led to Rome's decline.

Early Rome: The Rise of Monarchy

Ancient Roman historians record that Rome was founded by the legendary figure Romulus in 753 B.C. However, archaeologists have uncovered evidence that suggests Rome was a thriving town long before then. Scholars suspect that early Roman rulers were more like tribal chiefs than true kings.

The first-century B.C. historian Livy, along with other ancient Roman writers, records that there were seven kings of Rome. Their rules spanned about two hundred years, from 753 B.C. to 509 B.C. The first three kings are probably legendary. It is also possible that there were more than seven kings, and any information about them has been lost. Of these seven kings, very little is known. Even ancient Roman historians admitted that much of the information they had was based on myths and legends.

According to these accounts, the first king, Romulus, is said to have founded Rome. The second king, Numa Pompilius, enjoyed a calm and peaceful reign. However, the third king, Tullus Hostilius, was a warlike monarch who defeated the nearby Latin settlement of Alba Longa. The fourth king, Ancus Marcius, is said to have built the first bridge across the Tiber River. He also founded the important seaport city of Ostia, at the mouth of the Tiber.

The next three kings were Etruscans. There are no records that explain exactly how Etruscans became leaders of Rome. The first of these Etruscan kings, Lucius Tarquinius Priscus, conducted war throughout the area, but he also built Rome's first sewer, the Cloaca Maxima. The next Etruscan king, Servius Tullius enlarged Rome and built a wall around the city, protecting it from invaders. He also oversaw the construction of new buildings and temples. The seventh king, Lucius Tarquinius Superbus, was extremely unpopular with the Roman people. Eventually, he was exiled from Rome, ending the era of monarchs.

The Seven Kings of Rome

Romulus

Numa Pompilius

Tullus Hositilius

Ancus Marcius

Lucius Tarquinius Priscus

Servius Tullius

Lucius Tarquinius Superbus

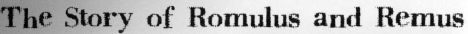

The Story of Romulus and Remus

According to the myth of the first legendary king, Romulus, he and his twin brother, Remus, were the sons of Mars, the god of war. As infants, they were thrown into the Tiber River. Found and cared for by a she-wolf and raised by a herdsman, the brothers sought to build a city that became Rome. Remus was killed, either by Romulus or by his followers, and Romulus became the first king of Rome.

Kings wielded great power in the early days of Rome. During this time, the Romans established the idea that the monarch had absolute power over the people. This power was known as **imperium**. The king created laws, served as the head of the military, and was the chief religious leader.

The king was also responsible for the growth of the city. Rome grew from an insignificant village into a powerful city by defeating and controlling surrounding territories. Wealth from the defeated groups began flowing into the city, encouraging growth and prosperity. New construction accommodated more people. As the ancient historian Livy wrote: "Meantime the City was growing by the extension of its walls in various directions, an increase due rather to the anticipation of its future population than to any present overcrowding."

The Republic: Consuls Wield Joint Power

When Tarquinius was overthrown, Rome already had a well-established senate and assembly, serving the king as advisers and lawmakers. Now these institutions became the leading powers of Rome.

The chairmen of the senate were known as **consuls**. They wielded imperium in much the same way as the king once did. Consuls commanded the armies in times of war. But their power was restricted. First, the term of consul lasted for only one year, guaranteeing that no consul could hold onto power for very long. Second, one consul could veto any action or decision made by the other one, so anything they did had to be mutually agreed upon. Third, the consuls were required to serve in the senate after their term of office was over, which meant that it was in their best interests to cooperate with the senators while they were in office.

The consuls and the senate held power in Rome for more than five hundred years, from 509 B.C. until the first century B.C. Then the Republic gave way to a new form of government, the Empire.

Roman Emperors and the Empire

By the last century B.C., there was unrest in Rome. Politicians struggled against one another for power as the senate tried to maintain its own control over the government. These political clashes resulted in civil war that further weakened the Republic. During this civil war, Octavian, a ruthless political and military leader, won an important battle at Actium in western Greece, in 31 B.C. This success ended the civil war. The grateful senate gave Octavian unprecedented powers.

Octavian was called Augustus, which means "the revered one." After years of bloody civil war, the senate and the people of Rome were happy to have a powerful leader. Augustus

Three Types of Rule

MONARCHY
(ruled by king)
(from 753-509 B.C.)

REPUBLIC
(ruled by senate)
(from 509-31 B.C.)

EMPIRE
(ruled by emperor)
(from 31 B.C.–A.D. 476)

won the respect of the senate by seeming to allow the old government to remain. Although Augustus kept up the illusion that the senate and the people were still in power, in reality, everything had changed. In just a few years, most of the power of the senate was transferred to Augustus. Soon Augustus wielded all of the power of the government. But he was careful never to refer to himself as "emperor" or "king." Instead, he called himself *princeps*, which means "first citizen."

The emperorship was passed down through Augustus's family. His successors were sons or other family members. Later, strong generals such as Vespasian and Hadrian, with no ties to the old Roman republican system, were elected emperor by the senate. The senate lost much of its power. Now emperors wielded total control over Rome.

Duties of the Emperor

The emperor was the commander in chief of the military, the high priest, and the source of Roman law. He supported massive building projects and other improvements to the city, such as bathhouses, theaters, and temples. The emperor was expected to be a patron of sports and other city activities. When an emperor died, he usually was proclaimed a god, and temples were built in his honor.

Emperors held on to their power through military strength and political loyalties, both of which could change overnight. In the forty-nine years between A.D. 235 and 284, for example, twenty-six military leaders seized control, throwing Rome into chaos. In A.D. 330, Emperor Constantine split the Roman Empire in two, creating a new capital called Constantinople, from which he ruled. From this time on, Rome fell into quick decline. In a little more than one hundred years, in A.D. 476, a barbarian leader named Odovacar assumed the title of king in Rome, ending the Empire.

Augustus was the first Roman emperor. His victory over Mark Antony and Cleopatra in the Battle of Actium helped him gain control of Rome.

Chapter II

POWER AND INFLUENCE OF THE ROMAN SENATE

As Roman civilization evolved from a monarchy into a republic and then into an empire, the government changed to fit the new needs of an ever-growing civilization. However, one major part of Roman government and life remained in place: the senate.

The Development of the Senate

Historians believe that the people who founded Rome probably had some kind of governing body of esteemed tribal elders chosen from the wealthiest and most respected clans. It was likely that these men elected or appointed the first kings. The senate advised and kept watch over the king to make sure that he followed local customs and traditions.

Originally, the senate consisted of one hundred men. This increased to six hundred during the Republic. By the time of the Empire, there were nine hundred senators. The historian Livy mentions this, writing, "He [the king] created a hundred senators; either because that number was adequate, or because there were only a hundred heads of houses who could be created. In any case they were called the patres in virtue of their rank, and their descendants were called patricians."

Patricians and Plebeians in the Senate

In the earliest days of ancient Rome, the people were divided into two main classes, the wealthy upper class called **patricians** and everyone else, who were called **plebeians**. Only patricians could be senators. Patrician status was **hereditary**. Patricians held important priesthoods, which gave them influence over the state religion. They were in charge of the law, and they controlled much of the army. They were also the largest landowners in Rome, although patricians made up only a tiny part of Roman society.

Most Romans were members of the less-privileged plebeian class. They were forbidden to be senators or priests. Plebeians could not hold public office and had no voice in lawmaking. For many years, plebeians were not allowed to marry patricians.

Not surprisingly, plebeians felt this was terribly unfair. They struggled against the patricians for decades, trying to win an equal place in Roman society. This struggle was known as the Conflict of Orders. The Conflict of Orders was not one single event. Instead, it was a series of events that scholars believe occurred between about 494 and 297 B.C. Eventually, plebeians gained more rights, including the right to marry patricians, the right to become senators and priests, and the right to become consuls.

The achievement of the plebeians created a new order of power in the senate and in Roman society. Power became

This sculpture shows a patrician, a member of the class of wealthy people.

Equites

In the days of Roman kings, there was a class of people known as *equites*. This class was made up of members of the cavalry. Only well-to-do Romans could afford to own and train horses *(equus)*, so equites eventually became part of a wealthy social class known as equestrians. During the Republic, this class rose to become a middle class of merchants and businessmen, many of whom had served as Roman soldiers and military officers.

Beginning in the second century B.C., members of the equestrian class could become senators. However, many equites preferred careers in business and commerce. Equites ran banks, lent money, collected taxes, and contracted for public projects, such as road building and supplying the Roman army.

based on political influence and wealth rather than on heritage and family ties. However, the overwhelming majority of senators were still from patrician Roman families, and the tradition of electing senators from the same pool of families remained the same.

Becoming a Senator

The senate served as an advisory body during the Republic, but gradually took on other important duties as well. Senators prepared legislation, handled finances, managed foreign relations, and supervised the state religion. The senate did not make laws, however. Instead, it issued decrees, which held the same power as laws.

Roman senators were not elected in the way that modern democratic politicians are elected to office. In the middle and late Republic, a Roman automatically became a senator when he became a **magistrate**, or government official. These officials

A Day in the Life of a Senator

The Roman writer and statesman Pliny the Elder (shown above) wrote a lyrical description of a day in his villa in the Tuscan hills. He wrote, "I wake when I please, generally at dawn. . . . I concentrate on what work I have on hand . . . then call in my secretary and dictate what I've composed . . .. About the fourth or fifth hour [8:30–10:30 A.M.] I go to either the terrace or the covered portico [porch] . . . think and dictate . . .then into my carriage to continue concentrating . . . then a siesta [nap] then a walk, and then I recite aloud a speech in Greek or Latin . . . then another walk, a rubdown with oil, exercise, and a bath. After dinner, reading of a comedy or music. Then a walk with my staff, some of whom are learned men. And so we pass the evening chattering on various topics."

The painting above shows Cicero (left, standing) giving a speech in the senate.

were elected by special political groups known as assemblies. In the Republic era, there were four Roman assemblies. Every male Roman citizen belonged to one of the four assemblies, based on such things as his social class and his wealth.

For hundreds of years, becoming a Roman senator was the pinnacle of ambition for many well-to-do Romans. To be a senator represented a great achievement personally and politically. Senators were among the most respected Romans. Many of them went on to become consuls and even emperors. Others retired from senatorial life to write or to enjoy their wealth on vast villas in the country. Until the fall of Rome, it was a point of pride for a man to say, "I was a senator in Rome."

Four Assemblies of the Roman Senate

Comitia Centuriata

In the days of monarchy, the structure of this assembly was similar to the structure of the military. During the Republic, it was made up of soldiers and other members of the military elite. This powerful assembly could only be convened by a magistrate with imperium. The members were divided into voting units called **centuries**, based on age and wealth. It had the power to declare war or peace and was responsible for electing the higher magistrates. It was also the highest court of appeals in the Roman legal system. It lost much of its power by the Empire period.

Concilium Plebis

To combat the power of the patrician class, the plebeians created this assembly in 494 B.C. For many years, it was restricted to plebeians only. It elected its own magistrates and other plebeian officials, and passed laws that applied only to the plebeian class. After 287 B.C. its laws applied to all Roman citizens, regardless of class.

Comitia Tributa

This assembly was made up of individuals from the various tribes of Rome. All Romans belonged to one of the thirty-five tribes that existed in Rome's earliest days. Members of this assembly were grouped according to the tribe they belonged to. It could be called to meet by consuls or other high government officials. It elected lower magistrates and served as a court of appeals. It also voted on legislation brought forth by magistrates.

Comitia Curiata

Originally, Rome was divided into thirty **curiae**, or wards. In the early days of the Roman civilization, this assembly was made up of men from these curiae. Little is known about the workings of this assembly, but it is believed that it had few legislative powers. By the late Republic, it met only for formal events and to bestow imperium, or power, to certain government officials.

Chapter III

PEOPLE OF THE ROMAN GOVERNMENT

During the era of the Roman Republic, the civilization expanded and conquered much of the known world. The people developed a complex system of officers called magistrates to handle the ever-growing responsibilities of a city that was fast becoming the center of the civilized world. Magistrates were the government officials of Rome and were elected by the assemblies.

Magistrates dealt with everything from religion and the courts to diplomacy and legislation. Anyone who was elected to a magistry office automatically became a senator, so becoming a magistrate was important for any man with political ambitions. Magistrates served one-year terms of office, and they could be reelected. With some exceptions, two magistrates held every office, similar to the way that two consuls ruled together over the senate and assemblies. This system prevented power from being held by one person alone. Two magistrates in the same office were known as *collegae.*

This relief shows Roman consuls. Consuls always were elected in pairs and worked together to prevent any one person from becoming too powerful.

Consuls and Praetors

When the leaders of Rome established the Republic in about 509 B.C., they had a problem. Rome needed a strong leader, but the people did not want a king. The solution was the creation of the consulship. Two consuls would be elected at the same time and would serve jointly. They would be in power for only one year. Because their term of office was so short, and because they had to share power with one another, it would be very difficult for a consul to abuse his power.

Consuls were the chief magistrates of Rome. The consuls presided over the senate and the assemblies when they were in session. Consuls created legislation and brought it before the senate and assemblies for vote. Consuls were also commanders of the Roman military, especially in times of war. The senate nominated candidates to the consulship, and the comitia centuriata voted on them.

The second-highest political office in Roman government was that of **praetor**. The praetorship was almost as prestigious and powerful as was consulship. Praetors were the highest judges in Rome, responsible for the law and the courts. The *praetor urbanus* handled the cases of Roman citizens. In about 241 B.C., Romans added another office, the *praetor peregrinus*, to deal with cases concerning foreigners. As Rome grew throughout the Republic era, more praetorships were created to handle the increasing burden of handing out justice to the people of Rome and its provinces. By about 80 B.C., Rome had eight praetors. Like the consuls, praetors were elected to one-year terms. Praetors issued edicts that had the force of law. These magistrates

Career Path: The Cursus Honorum

An ambitious young Roman who wanted a political career had a very specific path to follow. This path was known as the *cursus honorum*, or course of honors. It was put into law in 180 B.C.

His first step in the cursus honorum was holding either a military post or a minor civil office in the courts. He had to spend as long as ten years in the military or in the lower offices until he met the age requirements of the next step, the quaestorship. Every Roman had to be a certain age to be elected quaestor. The age requirement varied from twenty-five to thirty years at different times over the years. Becoming a quaestor automatically qualified the man as a senator.

Traditionally, there was a minimum interval of two years between magistries, so after that time was up he might turn his attention to being elected aedile. If he wanted to gain support and popularity, this was the public office to have. He could also choose to skip this office and run for praetor and later for consul or censor.

also had the job of holding special courts to prosecute corrupt governors, should the need arise.

Censors, Aediles, and Quaestors

The next series of government offices included three important positions, that of **censor**, **aedile**, and **quaestor**. These offices were not as politically powerful as consul and praetor, but they were all very important for the day-to-day running of the empire. These three offices were also the first positions that most Romans held in their political careers.

During the Republic, the position of censor became a prestigious and powerful magistry office. The comitia centuriata elected two censors every five years. The most important task of these magistrates was to count all of the Roman citizens. They wrote down the names, ages, and property values of each citizen, then kept

a register of the information. Each censor served for eighteen months.

They were responsible for large-scale public works projects such as building roads and leasing land that Rome acquired through conquest. One important censor, Appius Claudius, gave his name to two Roman public construction projects he oversaw. The Appian Way (or *Via Appia*) was an important roadway created during the Republic. The Appian **Aqueduct** (*Aqua Appia*) was the first channel to bring fresh water into Rome.

Censors were also the keepers of public morality. If a censor thought that anyone, even a senator, was behaving immorally, he could have that person removed or expelled. One of the most famous and strict Roman censors was Cato the Elder, who lived in the third and second centuries B.C. The Greek writer Plutarch recounts an instance when Cato expelled a powerful senator named Manilius from the senate for a public display of affection, writing that "Manilius, also, who, according to the public expectation, would have been next consul, he [Cato] threw out of the senate, because, in the presence of his daughter, and in open day, he had kissed his wife."

Most Romans saw holding the position of censor as vital to their political career. Censors dealt with all aspects of Roman life and regularly came in personal contact with many other politicians, senators, and magistrates. Holding the office of censor was an excellent way to become "known" in the right political circles.

Another office that regularly dealt with the Roman public was that of aedile. Originally, Rome had two plebian magistrates who were called *aedes*. Aediles were in charge of maintaining and repairing all of the public buildings and temples in Rome. They also took charge of Rome's food and water supplies, oversaw the markets, and managed Rome's public games and festivals. Later,

Careers After Leaving Office

When a consul left office, he could become a **proconsul**, or governor, of a Roman province. Provinces were lands and areas that had been conquered and were now under Roman rule. In some cases, usually during such emergencies as war, private citizens (men who were not magistrates) could be elected proconsul. One of the most famous examples of a citizen being elected proconsul is the story of Publius Cornelius Scipio, recorded by the Roman historian Livy. He wrote that in about 211 B.C.,

"it was decided that a commander in chief be appointed [to serve in Spain]. . . . Everywhere men were saying that no one dared to accept the command in Spain. Suddenly, Publius Cornelius Scipio, a young man barely twenty-four years old . . . announced himself as a candidate. . . .The individual voters were unanimous to a man in favor of entrusting P. Scipio with the supreme command in Spain. . . . He went on to lead Roman troops to victories in Spain."

the office expanded to include the administration of Rome's public buildings. After 367 B.C., two additional aediles were elected from the patrician class.

Although aediles weren't as politically powerful as other officials in the government, they came in regular contact with all facets of Roman society. Ambitious men, such as Julius Caesar, used the office to curry favor with the people. When he served as aedile in 65 B.C., he staged a number of large-scale public displays. According to the ancient writer Suetonius, "Caesar exhibited combats with wild beasts and stage-plays, too. . . . Caesar gave a gladiatorial show besides." For ambitious, wealthy men, serving as aedile was a perfect way to get publicity for future political campaigns.

The lowest office in the Roman government was that of quaestor. Quaestors were the financial officers of Rome. This magistracy was usually the first office that a young man would hold at the beginning of his political career. Quaestors were elected by the comitia tributa for one year. They maintained public records and the treasury and acted as paymasters for the military. The number of quaestors grew as Rome grew. By the end of the Republic, as many as forty quaestors were needed to manage Rome's finances.

Decline of the Magistrates

All magistrates, from the most respected consul to the lowliest quaestor, carried the burden of managing Rome. Throughout the Republic era, they represented the highest achievement of political ambition and power in Roman civilization. Any man who wanted political power or fame spent his lifetime rising through the ranks of Roman politics. To be a senator was, for some, the height of success. Others dreamed of being consul.

During the Empire, however, the powers of the magistrates diminished. With the establishment of an emperor, the senate and the other government offices slowly lost their influence. Instead, the emperor exercised most of the power himself. Gradually, many of these government positions disappeared or became honorary posts in the imperial court.

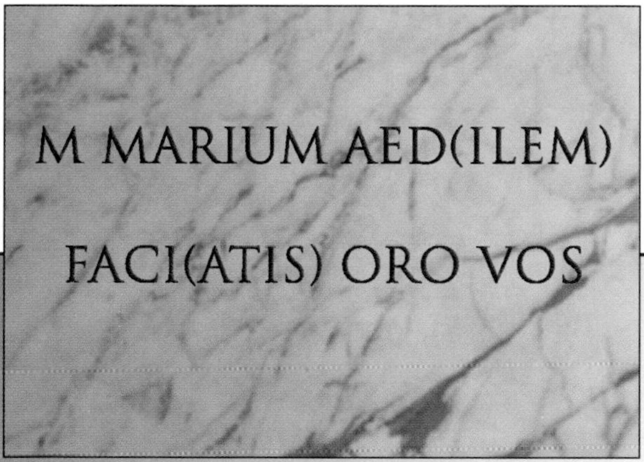

M MARIUM AED(ILEM)

FACI(ATIS) ORO VOS

MARCUS MARIUS:
ELECT HIM AEDILE,
I URGE YOU.

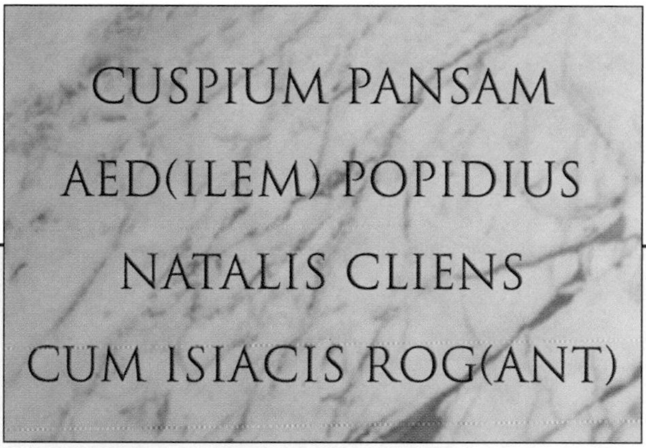

CUSPIUM PANSAM

AED(ILEM) POPIDIUS

NATALIS CLIENS

CUM ISIACIS ROG(ANT)

CUSPIUS PANSA FOR AEDILE:
POPIDIUS NATALIS HIS CLIENTS
AND THE ASSOCIATES OF ISIS
RECOMMEND HIM.

Political Advertising

In A.D. 79, the Roman city of Pompeii was buried beneath the ash spewed during the eruption of the Mount Vesuvius volcano. Large-scale excavations of Pompeii began in the 1800s and continue today. One of the most interesting archaeological finds at Pompeii is the graffiti scratched onto walls throughout the city, which includes some political slogans. Read for yourself some of the earliest known political advertising.

Chapter IV

SCHOLARS AND WRITERS

Roman civilization was not a culture that embraced learning for the sake of knowledge. Rome's educated elite did not concern itself with deep thinking about the human condition, science, or nature. But **philosophy** did occupy an important part of Roman intellectual life. The Roman way of thinking about the world adhered to very strict ideas of duty, honor, and a person's place in the grand order of the universe. This Roman worldview reached its peak of influence during the Empire, when a school of thought known as **Stoicism** became widely popular. Although Stoicism was created by the Greeks, it was the Romans who popularize it and spread it throughout the Empire.

Rise of Stoicism and Its Importance in Rome

The school of thought known as Stoicism was created some time in the late third century B.C. by a Greek thinker named Zeno of Citium, a city in Greece. Zeno taught in Athens beneath **colonnades** of columns. These colonnades were called **stoa** in Greek, which is where the term Stoicism originated. None of Zeno's writings survive, but other writers, both Greek and Roman, recorded parts of his philosophy. Gradually, the ideas of Stoicism traveled from Greece to Rome, where they were embraced.

The central idea of Stoicism was the idea of Logos. Logos was the rational order or meaning of the universe. To a Stoic, everything in the universe had an order and a meaning. Each individual life, every action, had its own purpose in the larger whole of history, from the lowest laborer to the emperor himself. Every person had a responsibility to perform the duties he had been born to do, to the best of his ability. Stoicism also preached that all people, regardless of wealth and position, were spiritual brothers.

Roman Stoics also embraced the idea that the greatest good was virtue. They struggled to do the right thing in all situations. There was good in every person, and true happiness was achieved when a person followed the goodness within himself and was content with his position in life. This way of thinking appealed to the Roman sense of duty, honor, and rational thinking.

Rome's Golden Age of Literature

Many Roman writers considered the reign of the emperor Augustus as the golden age of Roman literature. It was a time of peace and prosperity, and the arts flourished. Many of the greatest Roman writers and philosophers known today lived during this time, and many of the ancient writings that have survived date from this period.

The golden age of Roman literature also produced many great historians. The study of history was important to the Romans for a variety of reasons. Lofty tales of ancient heroes gave Romans a sense of pride in their heritage. Stories about the past

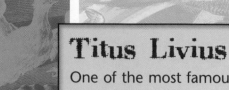

Titus Livius

One of the most famous Roman historians was Titus Livius, often called Livy for short. He was born in the Italian city of Padua, in about 59 B.C. His book, *The History of Rome from Its Foundation*, is considered to be one of the most important pieces of classical literature ever written. During his lifetime, Rome was at the beginning of the Empire, a time of great wealth and prosperity throughout the Roman world. Today, modern scholars know that much of what Livy included in his history was based on legends and stories he heard from others, so some of the information is of questionable accuracy. But it is still an excellent resource for stories of Rome and the people who lived at that time. His work is an epic account of an epic civilization.

could teach morals to future generations. History also reaffirmed Rome's place in the larger good of the universe, as the conqueror and defender of the world. The Roman writer Virgil summed up this Roman idea of history's importance to Rome in his epic poem, the *Aeneid*: "Remember, Roman, that it is for you to rule nations. This shall be your task, to impose the ways of peace, to spare the vanquished, and to tame the proud by war."

Other Roman Writers: Storytellers and Poets

Three important Roman writers created their most famous works during this time: Horace, Ovid, and Virgil.

Horace was one of the most influential Roman poets of his time. His most famous work, the *Odes*, was inspired by Greek poetry and praised love, wine, and the happiness of country life. His skill was in expressing simple ideas through lyric poetry.

Some consider Ovid's masterpiece to be his work titled *Metamorphoses*. It is a collection of verses based on Greek mythol-

In this portrait of the poet Virgil, he appears with two muses. The muses were the goddesses of artistic, scientific, and intellectual pursuits.

ogy, rewritten in a beautiful, elegant style. He also wrote *The Art of Love*, a book about sex and seduction for men and women.

Virgil is often viewed as the greatest Roman poet, and his work, the *Aeneid*, is considered to be one of the most important written works ever created. He modeled it after the Greek epic poems the *Iliad* and the *Odyssey*, by Homer. The *Aeneid* relates the story of how Rome was founded by a group of Trojan survivors. These survivors were led by Aeneas, who was the son of the goddess Venus and the mortal Anchises. The first six books of the *Aeneid* are modeled after the *Odyssey*, while the second six books follow the *Iliad*.

In a scene from Virgil's *Aeneid*, Aeneas is handed a shield right before his battle to win Italy. The shield, made by the god Vulcan,

Virgil in the Vatican

The great Vatican library in Rome is home to thousands of rare and ancient manuscripts. Some of the most important items in the collection are the works *Georgics* and *Bucolics*, known today as the "Palatine Virgil." It is a manuscript believed to have been copied in the fifth or sixth century A.D., making it one of the earliest copies of any classical Roman text and one of the oldest existing manuscripts in the world. The manuscript includes most of the text of Virgil's works. A few fragments of his writings are missing from the manuscript, including two out of the twelve books of the *Aeneid*.

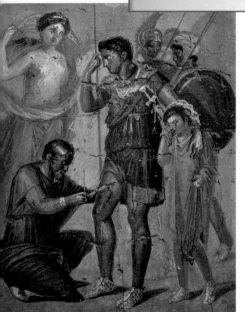

This is a painting of Aeneas, the central character in Virgil's *Aeneid*.

has the entire history of Rome inscribed on its surface. To the Romans, this scene perfectly illustrates the Roman view of life, the individual, and morality. "All these images / Aeneas admires on Vulcan's shield, given to him / By his mother, and, comprehending nothing / Of the events pictured thereon, / He felt proud and happy, and took upon his shoulder / All the future fame and glory of his descendants."

Decline of Roman Philosophy and Literature

Rome's golden age of literature declined after Augustus's death. At that time, Rome had a series of rulers, some good and some bad. Although there was warfare during Augustus's reign, the political unrest that began with his death marked the beginning of a time filled with more warfare, political maneuvering, and civil unrest.

The rise of Christianity also contributed to the decline of Roman thought. As Christianity grew more popular and more powerful in the later centuries of the Empire, Christian philosophy and ideas took root in Roman culture. The Roman ideals of duty, honor, individuality, and strength were slowly replaced by the Christian ideas of piety, devotion, sin, and modesty. By the fifth century A.D., the once-great Roman writers were forgotten, along with their works. It wasn't until the rise of the Renaissance in the fifteenth century, a thousand years after the fall of Rome, that the great Roman writers and thinkers were rediscovered by the world.

Marcus Aurelius

Arguably, the most famous Roman philosopher was Marcus Aurelius. He reigned as emperor of Rome from A.D. 161 to 180, but he spent most of his time fighting barbarian armies far from Rome. He was a well-loved emperor. As the Roman writer Eutropius said, "He conducted himself toward all men at Rome, as if he had been their equal, being moved by no arrogance by his elevation to the Empire. He exercised prompt liberality, and managed the provinces with the utmost kindness and indulgence."

He was also one of the most educated Roman rulers, schooled in philosophy, literature, and the Greek language. Aurelius loved philosophy and spent as much time as he could studying and writing. His greatest contribution was a series of writings called *The Meditations*, in which he discusses Stoic principles and his own thoughts about philosophy. Historians regard the *Meditations* as one of the most important documents to survive from Roman civilization.

Chapter V

SOLDIERS AND THE ROMAN ARMY

The Roman civilization lasted for more than one thousand years, from the traditional date of its founding in 753 B.C. to A.D. 476, when the last Roman emperor stepped down from the throne. During all of this time, Rome had a strong military. Warfare and the military deeply influenced Roman society and culture. Almost every Roman citizen was touched by warfare in some way, whether they served in the military, had family members who served, funded the armies, grew and prepared food for the troops, made clothing and armor, or housed the soldiers. War was part of the Roman identity. Romans thought of themselves as a strong, warlike people. They took pride in their military conquests and victories.

From the monarchy through the Republic era, Rome was almost constantly at war, expanding its lands and gaining political power. At the height of Rome's power, the army had

This mosaic shows Roman soldiers by the Nile River in Egypt.

conquered most of the European continent, from Britain in the north to North Africa in the south.

It was warfare—civil war—that eventually destroyed the Republic and began the Empire era of Roman history. During the Empire, the military continued to wage war and expand Rome's borders. By then, however, the army had become a force of occupation as well as conquest. Roman soldiers were needed to maintain control in the areas that Rome had conquered.

In the last years of the Empire, Rome's borders shrank, its power began slipping, and outside military forces began invading Rome's lands. Although the military tried to hold back the invading armies, ultimately they failed.

Origin and Growth of the Roman Army

Few details are known about the earliest Roman armies. Most of the information that exists comes from writers who lived centuries later. Archaeological finds also give some information. Together, these clues give historians an idea about the earliest Roman military forces

In about 1000 B.C., the Latins settled in villages in the hills above the Tiber River. By about 600 B.C., historians believe that these villages came together to create the city of Rome. The city needed some kind of military to protect itself from outsiders. At this time, there was probably no organized army. When there was a threat of war, the king called on local citizens to help defend the city. The first Roman army was probably a small force of Roman citizens led by the king. It is likely that the king enlisted the advice of a group of wealthy landowners. This group eventually evolved into the Roman senate. The king and these advisers made decisions about whether to go to war.

As the civilization and the army grew, the king needed

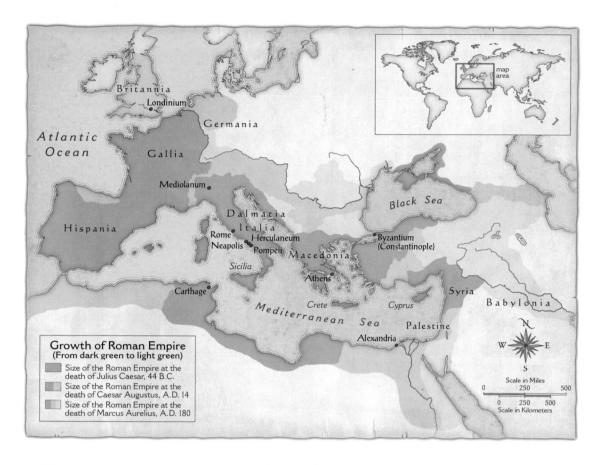

Growth of Roman Empire
(From dark green to light green)

Size of the Roman Empire at the death of Julius Caesar, 44 B.C.

Size of the Roman Empire at the death of Caesar Augustus, A.D. 14

Size of the Roman Empire at the death of Marcus Aurelius, A.D. 180

military commanders to help him. These commanders were known as **tribunes**, which translates to "tribal officer." In the early days of Rome, the army had between three and six tribunes. Later, that number increased to ten. Each commanded one thousand men, usually landowners, from each of the three tribes in Rome. These three thousand men were called a **legion**. The basic unit of a legion was a troop of one hundred men, which was known as a **century**. Each legion also included about three hundred **cavalry**, drawn from the wealthy class of Romans known as equites.

What a Roman soldier wore into battle depended on the time period in which he served. In early Rome, only the wealthiest soldiers could afford armor. Roman foot soldiers wore bronze breastplates, helmets, and leg armor. Weapons included spears and swords made of bronze. These soldiers also carried large, round shields made of wood or wicker that were covered with leather or metal. Soldiers who could not afford such fine armor and weapons used whatever they could find or make and carried spears, swords, and shields.

The Roman army organized itself into battle units called **phalanxes**. In a phalanx, soldiers stood closely beside one another in lines, one slightly behind the other, to create an imposing wall of shields and spears. The phalanx then marched forward and engaged the enemy. For about 350 years, from about 700 to 350 B.C., the Roman phalanx was very effective. It was extremely difficult to break through the wall of shields to fight an individual soldier. Also, once a phalanx began moving, it was almost impossible to stop it. Smaller, weaker armies were simply mowed down by the strong and heavy Roman phalanx. It was this army that was so successful in expanding Rome's borders and conquering neighboring groups in the early days of the civilization.

However, this type of warfare had a significant flaw. If the phalanx was broken in any way, it was destroyed. Any army that was strong enough to break through a phalanx would almost certainly defeat it. Once a phalanx was broken, most soldiers ran away, shedding their heavy armor and throwing down their weapons as they fled.

The most serious military disaster for the early Roman army came in 390 B.C. when a large army of Celts marched on Rome. They smashed through the large Roman phalanx that had assembled to defend the city. The Roman soldiers, terrified by the fearsome-looking Celtic warriors, were defeated. The Celts invaded and sacked Rome, although they did not stay to occupy it.

This disaster convinced Roman leaders that they needed a new idea for their army. In the years after their defeat, the Romans abandoned the phalanx. In its place they created a smaller, more flexible military unit known as a **maniple**. Maniples were small units that were independent of one another. They could fight alone or combine with other maniples to form larger units. Every legion was divided into these smaller maniples. The advantages of this kind of military formation were clear. Unlike the phalanx, which could only bulldoze forward on the battlefield, the maniple was flexible and could move anywhere it was needed to fight. If one maniple was defeated, others could fight on. The soldiers also began using shorter spears, which were better for close-range fighting. They abandoned their large, round shields in favor of smaller, oval shields that gave better protection.

These improvements transformed the Roman army. Because the maniple was flexible and effective, the Romans adopted it as their standard method of warfare throughout most of the Republic era. Using this type of warfare, the Romans conquered vast numbers of people and much land.

By about 100 B.C., the Roman army had grown tremendously. Soldiers had better armor, that included the **cuirass**, which was a type of body armor made of a front and back plate held in place with leather straps. Wealthy soldiers might also have chain mail armor, which was expensive to make and worn by only a few. At

This is the front part of a cuirass, a type of body armor.

An early second century A.D. marble relief shows Roman soldiers and officers.

that time, a brilliant military commander named Gaius Marius introduced some reforms that changed the army and in many ways made it even more powerful.

One of his biggest reforms was replacing the traditional maniple with a new kind of military troop called a cohort. Cohorts were groups of about 480 men, each divided into six centuries of eighty men. Cohorts were similar to maniples in that each was an independent unit that could act on its own during battle.

At this time, the standard legion was made up of ten cohorts, or about 4,800 soldiers. The smallest battlefield division was called a century, which originally consisted of one hundred men. Later, the number would vary from sixty to eighty men per century. By this time, most soldiers wore body armor called **lorica segmentata**, which consisted of strips of metal plates held together by leather straps and buckles. Soldiers also carried shields, swords, javelins, and sometimes daggers. These troops, along with a strong cavalry and a small navy, gave Rome its military strength throughout the Empire period.

Becoming a Roman Soldier

For young men from wealthy patrician families, joining the army was the first step in a respected political career. For others, it was a chance at having an honorable profession, earning decent pay, and gaining citizenship.

The Soldier's Oath

New recruits had to swear an oath. In the early days of the army this was a voluntary agreement, but later it became a formal oath. The Roman historian Livy gives some details of the military oath, writing that the "cavalry . . . and the infantry . . . used to swear of their own free will that they would not run away in flight or out of fear, and that they would not leave their ranks except to pick up their weapons or to look for them, and to attack an enemy or defend a citizen."

When a young man decided to join the military, he usually first secured a letter of recommendation from a relative or family friend who had served. One letter of recommendation from the third century read, "Priscus to Petronius, his father, greetings, I recommend to you a worthy man Carus, son of Aper. If he needs your assistance in any way, I beg you to honor me by helping him in so far as you feel proper."

Armed with his letters, the young man then presented himself at the local recruiting station for an interview, called a ***probatio***. Officials checked his documents and gave him a physical exam. If he passed, he became an official recruit of the Roman army. When everything was in order, the recruit received some traveling money and was sent to the unit to which he had been assigned to begin basic training.

Military Training

The best source of information about Roman military training comes from the Roman writer Vegetius, who wrote a book on military training in about A.D. 390. He describes a tough regime, including marching, running, swimming, jumping, and carrying heavy packs. Recruits used practice swords made of wood to learn fighting skills. Some recruits were chosen to train as archers. As Vegetius says, "About a third, or a quarter, of the young soldiers, that is, those who are found to be most suitable, should always be trained . . . with wooden bows and practice arrows."

Roman military training was difficult and thorough. The ancient Jewish historian Josephus described this training, saying that "every soldier is every day exercised, and that with great diligence, as if it were in time of war, which is the reason they bear the fatigue of battles so easily."

Once basic training was complete, the recruit was sent with his unit to the field to begin his tour of duty. This could mean facing a foreign enemy, manning a provincial garrison, or, in some cases, facing other Romans in civil war.

A Soldier's Life

A soldier's home was the army camp. Every evening after a day's march, the unit would pitch camp. Every Roman camp was identical. They were built so that two main roads intersected, with the general's tent near the intersection. Some soldiers dug a defensive ditch around the camp, while others set up tents, dug latrines, gathered wood, hunted food, and prepared for cooking the meals.

Discipline was a major part of a soldier's life. Every soldier acted only on command in battle and in camp. There was no bending of the rules, regardless of the excuse. If a soldier fell asleep while on watch, for example, he would be given a beating by every other solider who was put in danger by his mistake. This fear of harsh punishment is one reason that Roman soldiers fought so hard and so bravely during battle. As one ancient writer noted, "Therefore the men . . . often face certain death, refusing to leave their ranks even when vastly outnumbered, owing to the dread of the punishment they would meet with."

During the early and middle Republic, there was a specific "season" for warfare. Troops mustered and marched out in the spring and returned in the fall. As Rome became more powerful, the Roman military began fighting wars far from home, forcing the soldiers to be on duty for much longer than the summer

Remarkable Letters from Roman Soldiers

In 1973, two thin slivers of wood were found stuck together in a drainage ditch in a rural area near the Roman settlement of Vindolanda in Britain. When they were peeled apart, they revealed faint words! It turned out to be a letter to a Roman soldier, promising the lucky soldier that a package of shoes, socks, and underwear would be arriving soon.

Since then, more than 1,900 writing tablets have been found at Vindolanda, many of them written to and from the lonely Roman soldiers who were stationed there some time in the first century A.D. Some tablets include duty rosters and grocery lists. One reads: "Octavius to Candidus: I need money. I have bought 5,000 bushels of grain, and unless you send me some money, I shall lose my deposit and be embarrassed. The hides which you write about are still at Catterick. I would have already collected them apart from the fact that the roads are so bad that I did not care to injure the animals."

These letters are of great importance because they are some of the most revealing evidence of everyday life for Roman soldiers. They give modern scholars a glimpse into the world of the Roman military.

season. Men became professional soldiers, volunteering for duty for up to twenty-five years.

Decline of the Roman Army

The decline of the Roman army did not happen all at once. It deteriorated slowly over the course of about three hundred years during the Empire. Throughout this time, the army's influence and power rose and fell in fits and starts.

From about A.D. 30 to 180, the Roman army remained strong. Rome had five powerful and capable emperors during this time: Nerva, Trajan, Hadrian, Antoninus Pius, and Marcus Aurelius. Under their rule, Rome was stable and wealthy. This period of time in Roman history is known as the Pax Romana ("Roman Peace"). With the death of Marcus Aurelius in A.D. 180, Rome was plunged into a century of political unrest and economic catastrophe. Also during this time, enemy armies began attacking Roman holdings throughout the Empire.

The character of the army had begun to change. Instead of an army of conquest, the Roman army became one of control and defense. Soldiers trained to fight were instead posted to guard faraway provinces. Problems in the government meant that soldiers weren't always paid on time, or well, and this turned many people against a military career. More foreign-born men were recruited from the provinces, which meant that fewer soldiers had loyalty to

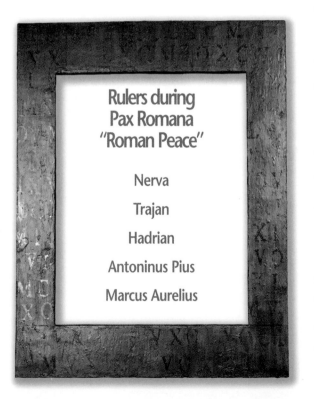

Rulers during
Pax Romana
"Roman Peace"

Nerva

Trajan

Hadrian

Antoninus Pius

Marcus Aurelius

Roman Helmets in Great Britain

In 2000, a group of amateur archaeologists in Great Britain stumbled on an important archaeological find—a hoard of ancient silver coins and the only silver Roman helmet ever found in that country.

According to experts at the British Museum in London, the coins and the helmet were found with evidence of a great feast. This suggests that the items were part of some kind of celebration or religious ceremony. What was more interesting to archaeologists was that the coins were probably made by an ancient Iron Age Celtic tribe known as the Corieltauvi. The silver helmet found with the coins was most likely a ceremonial helmet worn by a high-ranking officer during a parade or other celebration. Its discovery alongside the coins suggests that Romans were in Britain many years before historians had originally thought. If that is true, then this accidental find could rewrite British and Roman history.

Rome. Increased attacks from foreign armies, combined with the emperors' internal power struggles, all combined to gradually weaken the army.

Although the Roman army did have a number of military victories during this time, overall it was in decline. By the end of the Empire, Roman historians wrote that the Roman army was only a shadow of its former self.

Chapter VI

THE LIVES OF ROMAN WOMEN

Ancient Rome was a society dominated by men. According to the law, only men could hold political offices or vote in elections. Men had control over their families and sole legal rights to their children. Few ancient Roman writers wrote about women in their histories of Roman life. As a result, little information has been passed down to modern times.

However, women did have important roles in ancient Rome. Powerful patrician women, the wives of senators and emperors, influenced government. Plebeian women owned businesses and homes. Slave women took on the burdensome chores of day-to-day life. Although Roman writers rarely spent a lot of time writing about women and their role in society, they did occasionally tell stories of exceptional women. Roman historians and writers, including Cicero, Sallust, Catullus, Livy, Horace, Suetonius, Virgil, and Pliny, provide glimpses of the lives of upper-class Roman women. Modern archaeologists have unearthed wall murals and ruins that depict Roman women. Some of these archaeological finds include the murals in the Villa of the Mysteries in Pompeii and mosaics in Britain and Italy that depict women engaged in a variety of activities, including exercising and dancing. It is through these records that scholars learn about the importance of women to Roman society.

Women Throughout Rome's History

Almost nothing is known about Roman women from the earliest times. Most of the information that is known dates from much later in the history of Rome, during the Republic and Empire periods. It is from this time that modern historians have the best ideas about how Roman women lived and their role in Roman society. However, some clues about women in early Rome can be found in mythology and legends.

One such story is the legend of the Sabine women. The Sabines were a group of people who lived northeast of Rome during the time of the monarchy. The Sabines and the Romans fought one another until the Sabines were eventually absorbed into Rome sometime in the third century B.C. Legend says that early in Rome's history, the Romans attacked the Sabines and kidnapped their women. Later, when the Sabines tried to recapture the women, they discovered that the women had grown fond of the Romans, who were now their husbands. The legend says that the women placed themselves between the two armies to keep them from fighting, and battle was avoided.

This legend suggests that the Romans considered women to be both weak and powerful. They were objects to be controlled, but they were also respected. It was a conflicting view of women that would remain part of the Roman culture throughout its history.

Early Roman women were thought to embody all the values of the Roman culture, including courage, honor, and patriotism. They were trusted with passing these virtues on to their children, especially their sons, which was vital to Rome's future. In that way, women had a powerful role in family life within the household. A woman's fertility also gave her respect and power.

During the later part of the Republic and Empire eras, society's ideas changed, and women gradually gained more rights. They still could not hold political office or have any power in the government, but society began to accept that women did have rights, such as the right to divorce their husband, the right to own property, and the right to control their own money. Many male Roman writers of the time seemed to resent these new rights. Their writings reflect the conflict they felt about women and the powers they enjoyed in society. Some writers, such as the **satirist** Juvenal, were hostile toward women in their writings. Women were often judged more harshly than men, because society expected women to be virtuous and demure. By the end of the Empire, however, many wealthy patrician women wielded very real political and societal power. In many ways, these few women were more powerful than many lower-class Roman men.

Childhood and Marriage

Throughout most of Rome's later history, both girls and boys were under the legal control of their father. The father was known as the **paterfamilias**, or "father of the family." The father was the sole owner of all the property, and he had complete legal control over every family member. Although wives had few legal rights, in practice, most

women had control of the household. During the later Republic and the Empire, the wife enjoyed a certain amount of influence in the household. She usually had as much authority as her husband did over the children and the slaves.

Most Roman girls began learning how to run a household in preparation for marriage when they were about ten or eleven years old. The usual age for Roman girls to marry was about fourteen or fifteen, although girls could be married at twelve years old. It was common for a father to arrange his daughter's marriage, usually when she was very young.

It is uncertain exactly how much freedom the women of early Rome enjoyed. However, during the later Republic and Empire periods of Roman history, once a woman was married, she could usually enjoy a great deal of personal freedom within the relaxed atmosphere of Roman society. A Roman woman was seen as her husband's companion and partner, with opinions to be respected. Women could travel freely, shop in the markets, listen to open debates in the Forum, and attend dinner parties and other social functions.

Education for Roman Girls

Until about the third century B.C., there was little education available for Roman girls. They were taught household skills, such as spinning wool, cooking, and other aspects of organizing home

This wall painting shows a Roman wedding. Typically, Roman women got married around the age of fourteen or fifteen.

While rare, some Roman women became athletes.

life. From about the third century on, many Roman girls attended formal school along with Roman boys. Most girls usually left school when they were about eleven years old. Sometimes, wealthy families hired tutors to continue their daughters' educations, although most girls were not allowed to go on to higher study.

However, it was not unheard of for some women to seek advanced education. For example, in the book *History of Rome*, written sometime between A.D. 150 and 235 by the ancient writer Cassius Dio, there is a mention of a woman studying. The passage reads, "So greatly did Plautianus have the mastery in every way over the emperor, that he often treated even Julia Augusta [the emperor's wife] in an outrageous manner. . . . For this reason she began to study philosophy and passed her days in company of sophists [teachers]." Although this was not the experience of most Roman women, it does suggest that women were not completely prohibited from learning.

Women in the Workplace

Few ancient Roman writers mentioned the lives of the lower classes, so modern historians have little written information about plebeian and slave women. However, archaeological evidence shows that women played a vital role in the working life of ancient Rome. Stone carvings and funeral inscriptions depict women as nurses, midwives, weavers, and merchants. Many women worked alongside their husbands in other professions, such as ceramics and jewelry making. Mosaics show women athletes lifting weights and exercising. Others depict dancers, musicians, and entertainers.

Some successful Roman businesswomen paid for the building of public works, such as bathhouses or public monuments. Many surviving structures have inscriptions that record the women who sponsored their construction. In the excavations at Pompeii, for example, archaeologists unearthed the ruins of a civic building with an inscription honoring the woman who donated money for the project. It reads, "Eumachia, daughter of Lucius [Eumachius], public priestess, in her own name and that of her son, Marcus Munistrius Fronto, built with her own funds the porch, covered passage, and colonnade and dedicated them to Concordia Augusta and to Pietas."

The Face of an Empress

A circular object in the Altes Museum in Berlin, Germany, depicts a handsome family scene. The mother in the picture is Julia Domna, the empress of Rome. She sits beside her husband, Septimius Severus, and her young son Caracalla. Julia's other son, Geta, was once shown on the image, but his face was erased after he was killed by his brother when they were adults.

Julia Domna's face also appears on many Roman coins of the time. Only the most important and powerful people had their images struck on Roman coins. This suggests to historians that Julia was among the most important and influential women of the Roman Empire.

These small pieces of evidence give only a glimpse of the huge role that working-class women certainly played in Roman culture and society.

Women and Politics

Women were never allowed to hold political office during any time in Roman history. However, that is not to say that some women did not have political power. Most Roman women who enjoyed power in government were the wives, mothers, sisters, or daughters of powerful politicians, consuls, and emperors. They used their intelligence and influence over the men in their lives to shape Roman society.

One of the most influential and powerful Roman women of any period in Rome's history was Julia Domna. She was the wife of emperor Septimus Severus, who ruled from A.D. 193 to 211. Severus was a strong military leader who had had many war victories before he became emperor. As emperor, Severus was sometimes away from Rome, fighting rivals and waging wars against rebels in faraway stretches of the Empire. While he was gone, Julia Domna governed as empress, although she wielded her political power behind the scenes. In a sign of her power, she included her name along with his in imperial correspondence to the senate. She gained a reputation for being able to steer successfully through the dangerous political atmosphere of the imperial court. She sometimes traveled with Severus on campaign and was with him when he died in Britain in 211. She retained much of her power when her son Caracalla became emperor after Severus's death.

Another powerful woman was Livia Drusilla. She was the wife of Augustus, the first emperor of Rome. She stayed with Augustus throughout his years of power, becoming his most

Roman Women March in the Streets

In the years before 216 B.C., Rome waged many wars with neighboring cultures. Thousands of Roman men died in these wars. When they died, their wives and daughters inherited their wealth. Many Roman women became rich as a result. Some men did not like this. They resented the freedom and power that this wealth gave to women.

So in 216 B.C., Rome passed the Oppian Law. The law limited the amount of money a woman could have and ordered that any money held by single women, widows, and wards be deposited with the state. At first, women obeyed the new law. But later, they began to resent these restrictions. In 195 B.C., two tribunes, Marcus Fundanius and Lucius Valerius, proposed to repeal the Oppian Law. Senators and other influential men argued for and against the repeal. Roman women watched the debate closely.

When it looked as if the law was to be upheld, thousands of women took to the streets. The protest was described by the Roman writer Livy, who said, "This crowd of women was growing daily, for now they were even gathering from the towns and villages. Before long they dared go up and solicit the consuls, praetors, and other magistrates." Nothing like it had ever been seen in Rome before. Needless to say, the pressure was too much for the male officials. The Oppian Law was repealed.

trusted ally. He even left his personal seal with her while he was away, which was the most powerful "signature" of his power. By the time her son Tiberius became emperor, Livia was one of the most influential people in Rome. The Roman historian Cassius Dio described her power, saying that "she occupied a very exalted station, far above all women of former days, so that she could at any time receive the senate and such of the people as wished to greet her in her house; and this fact was entered in the public records. The letters of Tiberius bore for a time her name, also, and communications were addressed to both alike."

The role of women in Rome changed and evolved throughout the history of the civilization. Although there were thousands of Roman women, none of their voices can be heard today. They did not leave any written record of who they were, what they thought, or how they lived. Only a handful of women were mentioned by Roman writers, and they were usually upper-class women or important figures. Until recently, scholars and archaeologists paid little attention to the lives of women. Slowly, the lives of these women are becoming known, shedding new light on the role of Roman women in culture and society.

Chapter VII

PRIESTS AND THE ROMAN RELIGION

The Romans believed in the existence of many gods. They had a huge pantheon of gods and goddesses, each one with its own unique powers and personality. Most Roman deities were a blend of many different religious influences. Some gods and goddesses were introduced to the Romans by the Greeks. Other deities originally came from the Etruscans and from the early Latin tribes. In some cases, the original Greek or Etruscan name of a particular god survived. In other cases, the original names of the gods were forgotten or replaced by Roman names. That is why the Roman and Greek gods seem very similar, but have different names.

Jupiter was the supreme god of the Romans. He is the Roman counterpart to the Greek god Zeus. Jupiter protected Rome and ruled the heavens as the father of the gods. He was originally a sky god who controlled the weather, agriculture, war, peace,

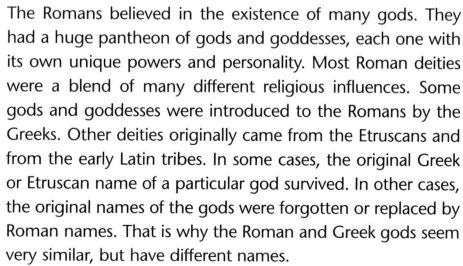

Jupiter, the supreme Roman god, was worshipped by thousands of Romans.

Dii Consentes (the Twelve High Deities)

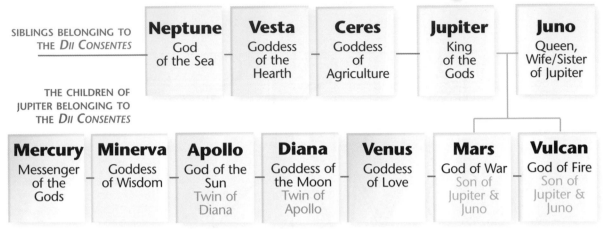

	Neptune	Vesta	Ceres	Jupiter	Juno
SIBLINGS BELONGING TO THE *DII CONSENTES*	God of the Sea	Goddess of the Hearth	Goddess of Agriculture	King of the Gods	Queen, Wife/Sister of Jupiter

Mercury	Minerva	Apollo	Diana	Venus	Mars	Vulcan
Messenger of the Gods	Goddess of Wisdom	God of the Sun Twin of Diana	Goddess of the Moon Twin of Apollo	Goddess of Love	God of War Son of Jupiter & Juno	God of Fire Son of Jupiter & Juno

THE CHILDREN OF JUPITER BELONGING TO THE *DII CONSENTES*

justice, and light. The Romans constructed beautiful temples to each aspect of Jupiter's powers. Each August 19, the Romans held a grand festival in Jupiter's honor as the god of agriculture. This festival was known as the **Vinalia**, or the Festival of Wine.

Juno was Jupiter's wife. Also known as Hera by the Greeks, Juno was the Roman queen of heaven and protector of women. As Juno was the guardian of females, Roman women believed that the goddess traveled with them through their lives, guarding them from harm. Her great festival was held each March 1, and it was called the **Matronalia**. The Romans built many temples in Juno's honor.

Mars was the son of Jupiter and Juno and was the god of war. To the Greeks, he was known as Ares. In the early days of Rome, Mars was the god of spring, nature, and fertility. Roman legend also says that Mars was the father of Romulus and Remus, the legendary founders of Rome. However, it was as the god of war that Mars was most revered by the Romans. Many temples to Mars were scattered throughout Rome. Sometimes a Roman army might gather in front of one of Mars's temples before marching off to war. The Romans also celebrated several festivals in his honor. For example, the **Armilustrum**, held each October 19, was a day when soldiers' weapons were ritually purified and then stored for the winter.

These and many other deities were all part of Roman religious beliefs. There is almost no information to tell us exactly how each deity was worshipped by individuals. It is thought that most people chose a god to be his or her patron deity. Each deity had its own group of worshippers, called a cult, that organized and participated in the festivals and celebrations in its honor. People also chose their patron deity based on what that deity stood for. So, for example, women might choose Juno because she was the goddess of women and the home. Soldiers might choose Mars, the god of war, as their patron deity.

Historians look to two sources for information about Roman gods and religion: the writings of ancient Romans and the archaeological evidence. Roman writers described many rituals, festivals, and other religious ceremonies, but they did not usually record the details of religion in the lives of most Roman citizens. Archaeologists have found many artifacts, such as temples and statues of the gods, that were likely part of religious rituals. By looking at both the writings and the artifacts, scholars can piece together how the Romans viewed religion and how they practiced it in their everyday lives.

Musicians often performed during festivals and celebrations.

Excitement of a Religious Festival

Roman writers described the excitement of Roman religious festivals. In *Geographica* by Strabo, written in about A.D. 20, he writes, "A festival is celebrated every year at Acharaca. . . . About noon, the boys and young men, nude and anointed with oil, take out a bull and with haste run before him into a cave."

In *Moralia*, written about A.D. 110, Plutarch wrote, "It's not the abundance of wine or the roasting of meat that makes the joy of sharing a table in a temple, but the good hope and belief that the god is present in his kindness and graciously accepts what is offered."

Origin and Growth of Roman Religion

Almost nothing is known of how the earliest Romans worshipped. There are few written sources that describe exact beliefs or rituals that were part of early Roman society. However, there are records that describe the various gods and brief mentions of certain festivals that were observed. These clues suggest that the early Romans did have a complex and sophisticated system of religion, temples, gods, and worship. Their religion was based on a mixture of fragments of rituals, superstitions, and traditions from a variety of sources, including the Etruscans and the Greeks.

As Rome grew, many temples were built and dedicated to the various gods and goddesses. Most temples were large, rectangular buildings with rows of columns along each side. Outside, there were usually steps and an altar. Inside, the temples usually housed a statue of the particular deity that the temple honored. In some cases, these statues were larger than life-size. Temples usually had a back storeroom where offerings were stored. However, no worshippers were allowed inside the temples. The Romans believed that the gods actually visited the temples and

The temple of Antoninus and Faustina dates to A.D. 141.

wanted privacy while there. Romans visited the temples to speak with the priests, to leave offerings, or to pray at the altars outside.

Roman Worship

Religion was not only part of the Roman culture, it was also a source of comfort and guidance for every person. The relationship between Romans and their gods was like a contractual agreement of mutual respect and responsibility. It was a person's responsibility to negotiate with the gods through an offering of sacrifice, vow, or prayer. The gods chose whether or not to accept that offering. If they accepted it, then it was up to the person to deliver what had been promised.

The Romans worshipped their gods in a variety of ways. The most important form of worship was sacrifice. There were many kinds of sacrifices. A common type was a **sacred vow**. A person or the state vowed to give the deity a gift if the deity granted the person's request. The vows were made either in private or in public. If

Romans believed that sacrificing animals was a way for them to honor the gods.

the deity did not fulfill his or her part of the agreement, then the person or the state was under no obligation to give the gift. If, however, the gods did grant the request, then the gift was given.

The gifts, known as votives, could be anything from a small figurine or coin to lavish items such as statues and temples. Most of the time the votive offerings were left at the temple of the particular god. Other times they might be placed in an area that was sacred to the god, such as a particular stream.

The most popular way to give a god a gift, however, was through the sacrifice of animals, such as pigs, goats, sheep, and oxen. Usually, the animal was killed and parts of it were left at the altar. The rest of the animal was cut up, cooked, and eaten by the worshippers. Many religious festivals included grand feasts in which the sacrificial animals were the main course.

Prayer was another common way that the Romans worshipped their gods. The Romans believed that there were specific ways to speak to the gods and certain ways a person must stand to address a god. For example, a common stance for prayer was to stand up, turn the face toward heaven, and raise the arms up with the palms upward. If a person did not stand right or if the prayer was recited incorrectly, the person had to start over. Romans prayed for much the same things that people might pray for today, such as good health, prosperity, or a good harvest.

The High Offices of Roman State Religion

It was not only individuals who worshipped the gods. Rome also had what was called the "state" religion. The Roman state religion was very similar to the religion practiced by ordinary Roman citizens, but on a larger and much grander scale. The state religion was guided by a group of government officials and administrators. Whenever war loomed, or when the senators needed guidance, or when the emperor wanted a sign from the gods, the officials were on hand to read the signs and interpret them correctly. Statewide religious feast days and festivals were also under the control of these officials.

The most powerful religious official in Roman society was the **pontifex maximus**. He was the leader of the **collegium pontificum**, the college of priests. The pontiffs determined the dates of festivals and kept records of when the main religious events were held each year. Plutarch wrote a detailed description of the duties of the pontifex maximus in his work *Life of Numa*, written in A.D. 75. He said, "The office of pontifex maximus, or chief priest, was to declare and interpret the divine law, or, rather, to preside over sacred rites; he not only prescribed rules for public ceremony, but regulated the sacrifices of private persons, not suffering them to vary from established custom, and giving information to every one of what was requisite for purposes of worship or supplication."

The first emperor, Augustus, served as pontifex maximus, the most powerful figure in the Roman religion.

The office of **rex sacrorum**, which translates to "king of sacred things," was established in the early days of the Republic to take over the religious duties once held by the Roman kings. The rex sacrorum was a special priest appointed for life to the office. The rex sacrorum was always the highest religious dignitary at any ritual— even higher than the pontifex maximus—but had less religious authority. By the time of the Empire, the office had lost much of its influence and had become an honorary position.

Flamines were officials who were appointed to serve individual state gods in Rome. Ancient Roman writers recorded that fifteen flamines served the "official" Roman deities, including Jupiter and Mars, and many lesser gods. The flamines were experts of the particular gods they served, specializing in the specific prayers and rituals for each deity. Because Jupiter was Rome's major god, the priest of Jupiter (known as the *flamine dialis*) was the most powerful flamen.

Auguries and Haruspices

The Roman people believed the gods communicated their will through various signs in nature. There were certain religious officers whose jobs it was to read and interpret the signs. One way that the Romans interpreted these signs was through the practice of augury, performed by a college of priests called **augurs**. Augurs were highly trained officials who were elected for life. They performed a ritual known as "taking auspices," which was reading the evidence of the god's will from the flight of birds and the feeding habits of sacred chickens. Auspices were taken before any major event, such as a sea voyage, war, or an important election. If the signs were favorable, everything moved forward. If the signs were bad, chances were that the event would end badly or even be cancelled.

An elderly man consults an augur, a person who was able to understand signs from the gods.

Another way the Romans interpreted the will of the gods was through animal sacrifice. Priests known as **haruspices** ("gut-gazers") read signs from the color, markings, and shape of the liver and gallbladder of sacrificed animals. Sometimes the haruspices interpreted bizarre or strange events, called **_monstra_**, such as the birth of deformed farm animals or other unusual natural phenomena.

Vestal Virgins

Among the most important religious officials in Rome were the Vestal Virgins. They were a group of six highly respected, sacred women whose duty was to maintain and care for the holy fire in the state temple of Vesta in the Forum in Rome. Vesta was the Roman goddess of the hearth and home. The pontifex maximus hand-picked the Vestal Virgins from the young daughters of respected patrician families. The girls, all between the ages of six and ten, were required to serve for thirty years. They trained as novices for the first ten years, performed their duties for ten years, and taught the next group of novices for their last ten years.

It was vital that all of the girls remain virgins throughout their lives as Vestal Virgins. If a Vestal Virgin was found to be guilty of losing her virginity, she could be buried alive as punishment, although this happened only a few times in Roman history. Vestal Virgins either continued to serve in the temple of Vesta after their time of service or they left to marry and start new lives.

Rights and Privileges of the Vestal Virgins

The Vestal Virgins enjoyed many honors and privileges that other Roman women did not have. The Greek writer Plutarch described some of these privileges in his work *Life of Numa*, saying that "they had the power to make a will in the lifetime of their father; that they had a free administration of their own affairs without guardian or tutor. . . . When they go abroad, they have the fasces [a symbol of power] carried before them; and if in their walks they chance to meet a criminal on his way to execution, it saves his life, upon oath being made that the meeting was accidental. . . . Any one who presses upon the chair on which they are carried is put to death."

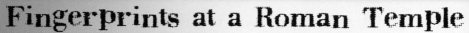

Fingerprints at a Roman Temple

In July of 2003, archaeologists made an astounding discovery in the area of Southwark, London, England. While excavating a Roman temple, workers found a small, sealed tin canister in an ancient drain. Inside the canister was some kind of ointment, with the fingerprints of its Roman owner still visible in the cream. Archaeologists were thrilled. Rarely do creams or ointments survive. It is unclear exactly what the cream was used for, although it could be some kind of cosmetic or medicine.

The temple area in Southwark is the first Roman temple complex ever to be found in the city of London and one of the most important Roman ruins in Great Britain. The canister of ointment is not the only important Roman artifact that has been found at the site. Archaeologists have also unearthed square temple structures, an inscription that is the earliest known naming of London (Londiniesi), and a life-size bronze foot.

This site provides rare and exciting evidence of organized Roman religion existing in London in the mid-second century A.D. The artifacts and buildings found in this ancient temple complex will give scholars a new look at the history of London and at the Romans who once lived there.

Decline of Roman Religion

Religion continued to play a vital role in the lives of the people throughout Rome's long history. But in the first century A.D., a new religion called Christianity came to Rome. At first most Romans tolerated Christianity. As Christianity grew and became more popular, Romans became more alarmed. Christians who refused to worship the state gods, which included the emperor, were put to death. One emperor, Nero, persecuted the Christians. For centuries, Christianity was viewed with fear and suspicion by the Romans.

Slowly, however, Christianity caught on. Emperor Constantine converted to Christianity and legalized the religion in the early A.D. 300s. Gradually, the old Roman beliefs in many gods was replaced by Christian concepts. The temples dedicated to the Roman gods were torn down or turned into churches, and the old religion died out.

Chapter VIII

ARCHITECTS AND ENGINEERS

The splendor of Roman architecture and construction is one of the most enduring aspects of Rome's civilization. The Romans are considered to be among the most efficient and practical builders ever. Rome was excellent at producing a variety of structures, including roads, aqueducts, bridges, temples, amphitheaters, and sewers. Many of these structures have remained standing for more than a thousand years.

Origins of Roman Architectural Knowledge

Most of the Romans' architectural knowledge was passed to them by the Etruscans and the Greeks. The Etruscans were the powerful culture that occupied what is now Italy during the Monarchy era of Rome's existence. Archaeologists have discovered many Etruscan structures showing advanced techniques, proving their expertise at construction. For example,

65

archaeologists have discovered ancient Etruscan roads, which leads them to believe that the Etruscans mastered the art of road building years before the beginning of the Roman civilization in the eighth century B.C. The Etruscans also understood the techniques of tunnel construction and channel building to carry water great distances. The Romans were also influenced by the Greeks. The Greeks had been building grand public buildings, such as temples, long before the Romans. The Greek practice of building enormous rectangular structures with soaring columns was later copied by Roman engineers.

During the first centuries of Roman civilization, architects simply continued the Etruscan and Greek methods of construction. Generally speaking, the Romans did not invent any new ways to build a structure. Rather, they took existing ideas and added their own ideas to them, creating a mix of old and new. This mix of ideas enabled the Romans to be innovative architects, even though most of the basic ideas they worked with had been developed by other cultures.

Roman Architects Combine Two Good Ideas

Of all the architectural innovations utilized by the Romans, the two greatest were in fact quite simple: concrete and the arch. When Roman architects combined these two simple ideas from other cultures, they revolutionized Roman architecture.

For centuries, Roman architects knew about concrete, which was a building material that was easy to make, was stronger than stone, and could be molded into any shape. It was made of cement and other materials, such as sand and gravel. Although the Romans did not invent it, they developed their own type of concrete. Historians dispute the time in Rome's history when it was first made. However, archaeologists have discovered Roman structures dating to before the second century B.C. that use their form of concrete for such things as foundations and some wall construction.

The arch was an important element in Roman engineering. The Romans borrowed the idea of the arch from the Etruscans. A typical arch began with two stone supports called piers. Wedge-shaped stones curved inward from the supports, meeting at the center stone on the top, called a keystone. This curve could support a great deal of weight. Another form of arch was known as a vault. A Roman vault was a three-dimensional version of the arch, mainly used for creating curved and domed ceilings. Again, the curved construction could support heavy loads, which allowed the Romans to build structures with very high ceilings.

The arch was a popular feature in Roman architecture.

By combining the strength of concrete with the strength of the arch and vault, the Romans could build enormous, soaring structures. By the first century B.C., the Romans had constructed many huge, magnificent buildings with concrete and the internal arch and vault system.

Roman Roads, Aqueducts, and Sewers

Today, the remains of two-thousand-year-old Roman roads stretch throughout many parts of Britain and Europe. Everywhere the Romans went they built roads. Roman roads were, for their time, masterful examples of construction and engineering.

To make the road surface, workers built a roadbed of stone, gravel, or clay. This bed was carefully made so that the road

One of the Romans' greatest architectural achievements was their system of aqueducts, which transported water over long distances.

would stand up to any traffic or weather without sinking or buckling. Then they cut blocks of hard stone such as granite into pieces about 16 inches (41 centimeters) across and 8 inches (20 cm) thick, and laid them into the bed. These blocks fit together perfectly to form a smooth surface. Roman roads could be more than 10 feet (3 meters) wide to accommodate two or three lanes of traffic. Builders constructed arched bridges that would be strong enough to hold up the road under even the most severe conditions.

Architects used the same care and expertise when building aqueducts. One of Rome's greatest achievements was the system of aqueducts that was built to bring water into most major towns and cities. Over a period of about five hundred years, from about 312 B.C. to about A.D. 226, eleven aqueducts were built near the city. Some stretched as far as 57 miles (91.7 kilometers). The most visible parts of the Roman aqueducts are the tall, arched structures called arcades. Arcades carried the water through certain areas, and they were built so that gravity would enable the water to flow through them. The Romans also built aqueducts in areas they conquered, such as Gaul, Spain, and Greece. In some of these former provinces, the Roman aqueducts are still being used today.

All of that water had to go somewhere once it arrived in Rome, so architects developed an elaborate system of underground sewers in the city. Rome's sewer system was a marvel of ingenuity in the ancient world. The sewers were constructed so that most of the wastewater from the bathhouses, fountains, and other public areas would drain into the Tiber River. The most famous Roman sewer is known as the Cloaca Maxima. It is believed to have been built during the time of the Roman kings as a way to drain the marshy areas of the Forum.

Egyptian Crocodile in a Roman Sewer

In 1999, archaeologists working in Gortyn, Crete, discovered a crocodile-shaped limestone waterspout buried in the rubble of an ancient Roman sewer. The crocodile had once been part of a Roman temple that was built between A.D. 161 and 180. At some point, the temple was left to ruin, and parts of it were used to construct other buildings. The fierce-looking crocodile, however, somehow fell into the sewer and was forgotten.

According to inscriptions on the temple, it was built by a man named Titus Pactumeius Magnus. Titus was a Cretan by birth, but he served as a government official of Egypt. He built the temple and dedicated it to the Roman emperors. The crocodile is the Egyptian style and is one of the earliest examples of Egyptian motifs on Roman temples in Crete. The discovery sheds new light on how art styles from other cultures may have influenced Roman architecture.

Vitruvius, Famous Roman Architect

Almost nothing is known today of the individual Roman architects who developed and constructed the great structures of Rome. Although it is certain that there were hundreds of skilled and educated men who designed the buildings, few records of them remain today.

However, one Roman architect is known to modern scholars, Marcus Vitruvius. He is famous for writing *On Architecture*, the only textbook on Roman architecture and building techniques to survive to the present day. *On Architecture* was written in 27 B.C. and is divided into ten books that cover designing such things as harbors, aqueducts, pumps, clocks, public buildings, private homes, and water supplies.

In the first chapter of the first book, Vitruvius details the kind of education a Roman architect should have, including knowledge of history, philosophy, and music; skills in manual construction; drawing skills; and even some medical knowledge. He goes on to describe the different elements of architecture and to give detailed instructions about construction.

Scholars believe that Vitruvius was a self-taught expert in architecture, combining his love of design with a variety of skills he thought a good architect should have. His work shows that he was extremely intelligent and knowledgeable about every aspect of architecture. He advises readers to choose "healthy" construction sites with good wind and not too much sun, for example. When constructing city walls, he shows an understanding of battle techniques so that the walls will be effective against a variety of attacks. He is even one of the first environmental architects. He advises that walkways be planted with green plants that are pleasing to the eye and healthy for the body.

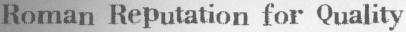

Roman Reputation for Quality

The Romans were renowned throughout the world for their buildings and the people who constructed them. A Greek writer named Strabo visited Rome in the last years of the first century B.C. and wrote of the architectural marvels of the city, saying, "The Romans have made provision above all for those things that the Greeks have slighted: the construction of roads and aqueducts, and of sewers capable of washing away the city's waste into the Tiber. And they have laid roads throughout the country, cutting through hills and building up over valleys so that their wagons can carry veritable cargoes. Their sewers, covered with vaulting of cut stone, offer in places a channel hay carts could pass through. So much water is piped in through aqueducts that it flows like streams through the city and its drains."

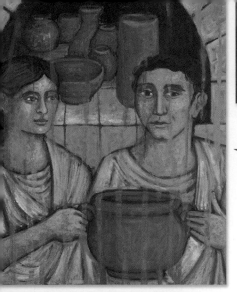

Chapter IX

WORKING-CLASS ROMANS

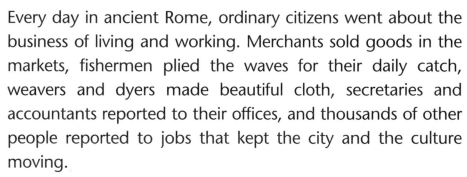

Every day in ancient Rome, ordinary citizens went about the business of living and working. Merchants sold goods in the markets, fishermen plied the waves for their daily catch, weavers and dyers made beautiful cloth, secretaries and accountants reported to their offices, and thousands of other people reported to jobs that kept the city and the culture moving.

Very little is known about the lives of the working classes of Rome. Few existing Roman texts mention them at all. One reason for this is that most of the ancient Roman writings that survive were written by the elite. Most upper-class Romans considered working Romans to be beneath them, worse than slaves because they were "enslaved" by the wages they earned for their work. The Roman writer Cicero spoke for most wealthy Romans when he wrote, "Unbecoming to a gentleman, too, and vulgar are the means of livelihood of all hired workmen whom we pay for mere manual labor . . . for in their case the very wage they receive is a pledge of their slavery."

The working class did not write about themselves in the same way that the Roman elite recorded their upper-class lives. Instead, historians and archaeologists must look at such things as tombs, paintings, and other ancient artifacts for clues about the lives of the Roman working class.

Who Were the Working-Class Romans?

Many of the men and women who lived and worked in Rome were slaves. Wealthy Romans might own hundreds of slaves who did all the work of running a large household. Slaves took care of every aspect of maintaining the land, houses, and crops. Men did farm chores, cared for the animals, weeded and planted the crops, and made all of the tools and materials needed for farm-work. Women cooked, cleaned, wove cloth and made clothes, cared for children, and also did many farm chores.

Working-class Romans helped sustain the civilization by providing much-needed goods and services.

In the urban areas, most of the workers in city offices and businesses were slaves. Slaves worked as clerks, secretaries, and assistants to Roman magistrates. They were employed to maintain private homes. Slaves did a great deal of the difficult city labor such as rebuilding and maintaining streets, sewers, and public structures.

This stone carving shows what a typical merchant's stand looked like. This merchant sold groceries.

Newly freed slaves also made up a large segment of the working classes. These people were the lucky slaves who were able to gain their freedom, either by purchasing it or by being freed by their masters. These people generally were literate and had some money. They might have learned a trade while in slavery, such as shoemaking or weaving.

Freeborn Romans were also a part of this class. The freeborn were people who had not been born into slavery, but whose families were poor or of the plebeian class. During the late Republic and the Empire thousands of foreign-born free people poured into Rome from the provinces and lands that Roman armies had conquered. They settled in Rome and established shops and businesses. Young men in a family might join the Roman army, becoming Roman citizens after their tour of duty was over. In one or two generations, these working-class families would be Roman citizens in their own right.

Where the Working Class Worked

Excavations in the city of Pompeii reveal how working-class Romans lived. Narrow streets are lined on either side with modest buildings. Most of the buildings were owned by wealthy Romans who divided the street-level first floors into shops and rented them out. Some of the shops were factories where slaves might mass-produce such things as tools, clothing, equipment, armor, or building materials for sale. Others were take-out restaurants in which patrons could order a quick meal of fish, bread, and wine from a bar that faced the busy street.

Archaeological Evidence

Since archaeologists and historians can rarely look to written evidence for information about Rome's working class, they use archaeological evidence to reconstruct the lives of ordinary working-class Romans. They also look to Roman cities such as Pompeii, which was buried by the eruption of Vesuvius in A.D. 79, for clues as to how these Romans lived.

One example of this is the story of a Roman lamp maker named Faustus. He lived sometime in the first century B.C. His lamps were beautiful and well made. He had a good reputation for the quality of his work, which was traded throughout the Roman Empire, particularly in the eastern areas of Egypt and Libya. Historians know his name because he signed the bases of his lamps.

Nothing else is known of Faustus's life, however, such as where he lived or any other details. But archaeologists have found Faustus's lamps at sites throughout the Middle East,

Where to Buy the Best

Cato the Elder, in his work *On Farming*, gives a comprehensive list of where to purchase the best merchandise. Although he only mentions one craftsman by name, it is clear that all these items were probably made by working-class Romans and traded throughout Rome's provinces.

Cato says to "Buy tunics, togas, cloaks and blankets, and clogs at Rome. Hoods and ironware (scythes, spades, mattocks, axes, harness, and chains) at Cales and Minturnae, spades at Venafrum. Carts and sledges at Suessa and in Lucania. At Rome and in Alba, vats and basins; roof tiles made in Venafrum. Rome-made plows are good for heavy soil, Campania's for dark soil. Rome's yokes are the best. Detachable plowshares will do the best. Oil mills at Pompeii and in Nola at the shop of Rufrius. Rome for nails and locks, hooks, oil vats, water pitchers, and wine jugs, in fact all sorts of bronze, in Capua and Nola. Capua's Campanian baskets are good; at Capua also ropes for hoists and all kinds of cordage."

indicating how widespread his handiwork was. He must have been well respected for his work, because so many people wanted to own his lamps. He was probably wealthy, because he had the resources either to maintain a large trade business or to set up workshops around the Empire. The evidence suggests that he was a prosperous Roman working-class craftsman.

One of the few working-class Romans who is mentioned in ancient writings is a grammar teacher named Quintus Remmius Palaemon. The Roman writer Suetonius mentioned Quintus in his work *De Grammaticis*. Quintus was an intelligent, educated man who was a slave. He somehow won his freedom, then went on to teach grammar in Rome. According to Suetonius, Quintus wrote a book on grammar (now lost) that was used as a textbook

The ruins of the city of Pompeii provided more information on working-class Romans. This photograph shows some of the artifacts that have been uncovered there.

in his own lifetime. Teaching was one of the few professions that the elite Roman classes respected, so it was not unusual for Suetonius to write about Quintus.

Archaeologists and historians also look to the ruins of the Roman city Pompeii for evidence of the lives of working-class Romans. When Pompeii was buried by the ash spewed from the volcano, the city was preserved, essentially freezing it in time. Taverns and shops filled the streets of Pompeii, including restaurants, bars, bakeries, food stalls, and shops selling everday items, such as pottery. Archaeologists have discovered thousands of artifacts, including bowls still of food, and loaves of bread still in large ovens, that show the kind of merchandise the working class made and sold.

A Roman Baker's Tomb

Marcus Vergilius Eurysaces was a wealthy and prosperous baker. He had been elected to government office, and he probably had contracts with the city to provide bread. When he died in 15 B.C., a magnificent tomb was built—in the shape of a baker's oven. Archaeologists have studied his tomb and its inscriptions to reveal how one working-class Roman lived.

His name indicates that he was once a slave and somehow achieved his freedom. If he had died a slave, he would have only had only one name. The third name indicates he was a Roman citizen, and therefore free.

The tomb has two sections. The lower part is built to resemble the part of the oven where the fire was built. The upper section includes a series of holes where the bread was baked. In between the sections is an inscription that reads "This tomb belongs to Marcus Vergilius Eurysaces, baker, contractor, government official."

Chapter X

SLAVES AND SLAVERY

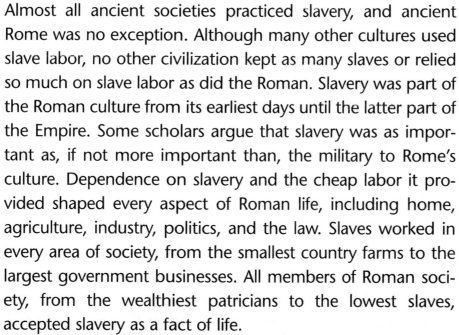

Almost all ancient societies practiced slavery, and ancient Rome was no exception. Although many other cultures used slave labor, no other civilization kept as many slaves or relied so much on slave labor as did the Roman. Slavery was part of the Roman culture from its earliest days until the latter part of the Empire. Some scholars argue that slavery was as important as, if not more important than, the military to Rome's culture. Dependence on slavery and the cheap labor it provided shaped every aspect of Roman life, including home, agriculture, industry, politics, and the law. Slaves worked in every area of society, from the smallest country farms to the largest government businesses. All members of Roman society, from the wealthiest patricians to the lowest slaves, accepted slavery as a fact of life.

No one is sure how many slaves lived in Rome at any given time. Some historians estimate that at slavery's height, probably during the latter centuries of the Republic, one out of every three people in Rome was a slave. It is estimated that

Slaves provided the labor to run many businesses, such as the bakery shown here, and the estates of wealthy Romans.

between about 200 B.C. and A.D. 200, Rome had more slaves and was more dependent on slave labor than at any other time in its history. In many ways Roman civilization, as the Romans knew it, could not have existed without slavery. The style and quality of life in Roman culture depended on slave labor.

The Roman Idea of Slavery

The idea of slavery in Rome was very different from the modern concept of slavery. Today, slavery is thought of as a group of people held in bondage against their will, with no way of escape. The Roman concept of slavery was vastly different. Slaves had few legal rights, but they were acknowledged as human beings with feelings and lives of their own. Slaves could buy their own freedom, becoming freedmen and freedwomen with more rights in society. Of course, slaves still had to obey their masters, and there were many cruel Romans who whipped, starved, and sometimes killed their slaves. But there were also kind Romans whose slaves remained faithful and loving companions for their whole lives.

The main function of slaves was to do all of the day-to-day work of running society. From about the second century B.C. onward, all slaves were either public or private slaves. There were two kinds of public slaves, the **servi publici** and the **servi privati**. Servi publici were owned by the state, by individual towns, or, during the Empire, by the emperor. They usually had dangerous or difficult jobs, such as working in mines or quarries. Some had better jobs on the staffs of state priests, consuls, or magistrates. Others were used to construct temples and other public structures, or to maintain roads. Servi privati worked in individual trades or industries as assistants, apprentices, or laborers for their masters, who owned or managed the businesses.

Private slaves also belonged to one of two classes, the **familia urbana** or the **familia rustica**. Familia urbana were household workers. They included housekeepers, maids, cooks, and bakers. Literate and intelligent slaves might have jobs as personal secretaries and bookkeepers for the household. Slaves who worked outside the house were familia rustica. These included farmworkers, herdsmen, or gatherers in the fields.

It was usually preferable to be a public slave in Rome than a private slave. Public slaves had more personal freedom and in some cases could own property. They were also rarely sold. Private slavery, on the other hand, could be either wonderful or horrible. Slave owners could, by law, treat their slaves any way they chose. Punishments such as beatings or even death were not uncommon, although most Romans believed in treating their slaves humanely.

Becoming a Slave

Before about the third century B.C., only very rich patricians owned a great number of slaves. Plebians, such as farmers or small businessmen, managed their affairs with the assistance of their families and perhaps one or two slaves.

A person might become a slave in a variety of ways. The most common way was through warfare. In the early days of Roman civilization, slaves were captured from nearby defeated groups, such as the Etruscans. During the rise of the Republic, Rome began conquering large territories and increasing its power through warfare. Part of the spoils of war were slaves from the cultures and countries now under Rome's control. Thousands of slaves were brought into Rome from Spain, Greece, Macedonia, Asia Minor, and later from Gaul and Britain. Piracy was also a common way for Rome to acquire slaves.

Another way to become a slave was to be born one. The children of slaves automatically became slaves themselves. For wealthy patrician slave owners, this method of increasing their slave holdings was much cheaper, and therefore preferable, to buying foreign slaves on the open market. During the Empire period, acquiring slaves this way became the chosen method.

Another steady supply of slave children was the large number of infants cast out and left in the streets to die. It was common for poor Roman families to abandon infants, usually girls. Many of these children were rescued and made slaves. Although it was illegal to put a freeborn Roman child into slavery, it was all but impossible to prove that an abandoned infant was freeborn.

After defeating an enemy, the Romans took some of the enemy soldiers to become slaves.

Child slaves, especially beautiful ones, were especially sought after by rich patricians as status symbols.

In some cases, the punishment for committing certain crimes was being sold into slavery, although this punishment was usually reserved for plebeians and other lower-class Romans. Patricians and powerful Romans were rarely, if ever, sold into slavery as punishment.

In rare cases, a person could sell himself or herself into slavery. Although this was very uncommon, it did happen. A person might be forced to sell himself into slavery as a way to pay off debts. Others might do it as a way to better their lives. Slaves were usually given food, clothing, shelter, and the basic necessities of life. For poor Romans, the lower-class freeborn, noncitizens, or people who were in otherwise desperate situations, slavery could look much better than their own bleak lives. Later, if they were fortunate enough to eventually buy their freedom, they would have achieved a much better position.

How a Good Slave Should Act

The Roman playwright Plautus, in about 200 B.C., described how many Romans expected their slaves to serve them, then went on to explain the kinds of punishment a slave might expect if he or she did not work hard enough. Plautus says, "This is the proof of a good servant: he must take care of his master's business, look after it, arrange it, think about it; when his master is away, take care of it diligently just as much as if his master were present. . . . Stripes, fetters, the mill, wariness, hunger, bitter cold—fine pay for idleness."

Meet the Gladiators

Gladiators were one of the most famous aspects of Roman society. They were an important part of Roman culture from the earliest days of the Monarchy until the end of the Empire in the fifth century A.D.

The earliest gladiators existed during Rome's Monarchy period. Historians believe that the first gladiatorial combats were conducted as part of funerary rituals. It is possible that these first gladiators were prisoners of war who were forced to fight to the death. By the time of the Republic, government officials and candidates for office would stage elaborate gladiatorial games for public entertainment and political gain. For example, when Julius Caesar ran for the office of aedile in 65 B.C., he held a massive celebration that included hundreds of gladiatorial combats.

Throughout most of the Empire era, gladiatorial games were held as public spectacles for all Romans and as private entertainment paid for by wealthy Romans for the amusement of their friends and colleagues. When the grand Coliseum was completed in A.D. 80, for example, the emperor Titus opened it with a spectacular one-hundred-day celebration that included gladiatorial games.

Becoming a Gladiator

Throughout the Monarchy and into the Republic eras, Roman gladiators were slaves, convicted criminals, or prisoners of war who had been condemned to death. In some cases, being sold as a gladiator was a way that slave owners punished their slaves for some wrongdoing. By the time of the Empire, the popularity of gladiatorial games had grown so much that new sources of gladiators sprang up. Roman citizens, freedmen, and even members of the patrician class chose to become gladiators. They were known as **_auctorati_**, those who voluntarily sought the gladiator lifestyle. They signed on for a fee and swore an oath of absolute

A gladiator looks to the crowd to determine whether or not he should kill his opponent.

submission. By the end of the Republic, about half of the gladiators were auctorati. Rome also had female gladiators at the end of the Empire. For example, the Roman emperor Septimius Severus, who ruled from A.D. 193 to 211, allowed women to be gladiators.

Gladiators trained in special schools, most of which were owned by the Roman government. Historians think there were at least four gladiatorial schools in Rome. One such school, Capua, was believed to have been started during Rome's Monarchy period. Another popular gladiatorial school was located in Pompeii.

A **lanistae**, or trainer, drilled the gladiators in gymnastics, strength training, and endurance. A gladiator's training was much like military training—hand-to-hand combat, weapons handling, and sword fighting. Eventually, a gladiator would choose a particular weapon to specialize in, and would then get specific training in using that weapon.

Throughout the Republic and Empire eras, there were three main types of gladiators: **eques**, **essedarii**, and **galli**. The eques were horsemen. The essedarii were charioteers. Galli fought with heavy weapons, and they were further divided by the specific kinds of weapons they used.

Once they were trained, gladiators would perform at festivals and other functions. Sometimes famous gladiators might go on tour, performing in amphitheaters

This mosaic shows gladiators fighting. Sometimes they fought only with their hands (top), and at other times they used weapons (below).

Female Gladiator Found in Britain

In 1996, archaeologists working in the Southwark section of London, England, unearthed the remains of a young woman. She was about twenty years old when she died. She was buried with a number of items that indicate that she was probably a female Roman gladiator.

Workers found a dish decorated with the image of a fallen gladiator, along with other pieces of pottery that showed gladiatorial scenes and symbols. The woman was also buried with lamps decorated with the Egyptian god Anubis, who was linked to the Roman god Mercury. This is an important connection, because Roman slaves dressed as Mercury were sometimes used to remove dead gladiators from amphitheaters.

Archaeologists found other evidence that the woman was a popular figure. Remains of an elaborate feast that included dates, almonds, figs, and a dove suggest that the woman was important in the community. All of these clues are strong evidence that the woman was a gladiator. If so, this discovery would be the first female Roman gladiator grave to be found anywhere in the world.

throughout the Roman provinces. Gladiators were not paid a wage for their work. Instead, they received generous prize money for winning. In some cases, popular gladiators had wealthy patrons who paid their expenses and gave them an allowance. Some gladiators made a great deal of money and became rich.

The fashion for gladiatorial combats lasted until the end of the Empire. When Christianity took hold, gladiatorial combat was strongly denounced by Christian leaders. It was regarded as a pagan form of entertainment and a symbol of Rome's corruption and excess. By A.D. 400, the last of the gladiatorial schools were closed. But combats continued until 404, when Emperor Honorius abolished them completely.

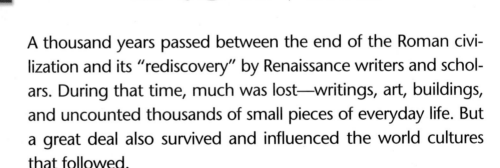

Chapter XI

LEGACY OF ANCIENT ROME

A thousand years passed between the end of the Roman civilization and its "rediscovery" by Renaissance writers and scholars. During that time, much was lost—writings, art, buildings, and uncounted thousands of small pieces of everyday life. But a great deal also survived and influenced the world cultures that followed.

Rome influenced the modern world in two main areas: law and language. The Roman ideas of trial by jury and impartial justice were adopted by European law courts in later centuries. In the sixth century, the Romans compiled a massive book known as the Justinian Code. It contained hundreds of Roman statutes and comments on Roman law. The Justinian Code strongly influenced future European justice systems, including those of Germany and France. Today, many aspects of the American legal system can trace their origins to ancient Roman law.

World languages were also influenced by Rome. Latin, the language of Rome, continued to be the language of scholars long after the height of ancient Roman civilization. Latin was slowly adapted by a wide variety of other people and evolved into the group of languages known as the Romance languages. This includes French, Spanish, Portuguese, and Italian. Almost one-third of all English words have Latin origins. Today, Latin is the language of science and medicine. It is used to name most medical conditions and species of life on Earth. It is also the language of the Roman Catholic Church.

In addition, the Romans originated many other modern institutions and adopted others from the Greeks, Persians, Egyptians, and other cultures. As author Anthony Kamm in his book, *The Romans*, describes, "Banking, public hospitals, the postal system, the daily newspaper, the fire service, central heating, glass windows . . . sanitation, drainage and sewers, social benefits and public education are all Roman institutions."

In many ways, Rome lives on through the archaeology of its culture, the beauty of its art and architecture, the strength of its ideas about law and justice, and its language and literature. These fragments of Roman civilization continue to affect the world today.

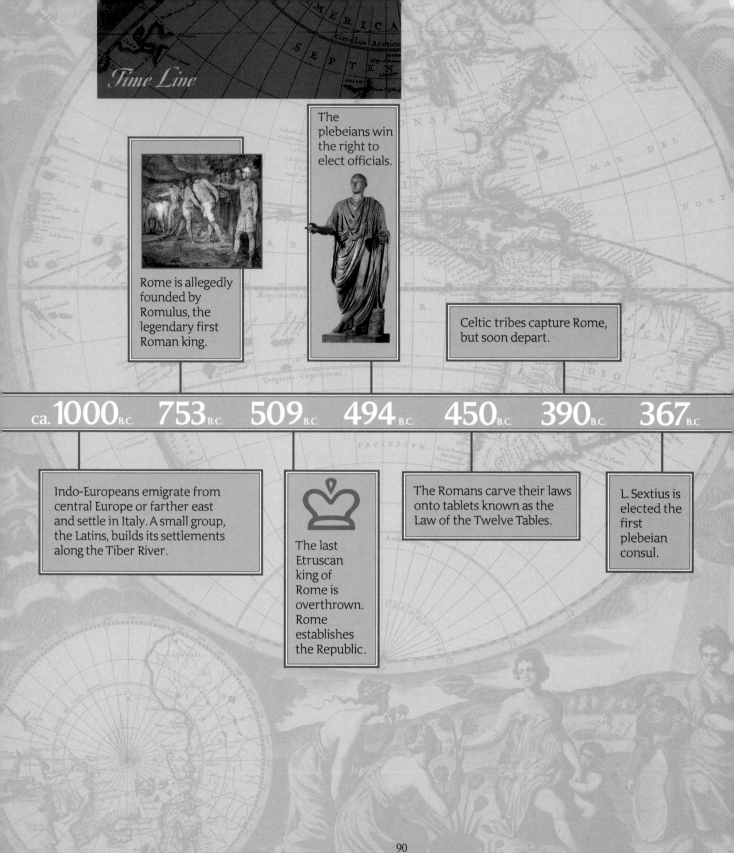

The plebeians win the right to elect officials.

Rome is allegedly founded by Romulus, the legendary first Roman king.

Celtic tribes capture Rome, but soon depart.

ca. **1000**B.C.   **753**B.C.   **509**B.C.   **494**B.C.   **450**B.C.   **390**B.C.   **367**B.C.

Indo-Europeans emigrate from central Europe or farther east and settle in Italy. A small group, the Latins, builds its settlements along the Tiber River.

The last Etruscan king of Rome is overthrown. Rome establishes the Republic.

The Romans carve their laws onto tablets known as the Law of the Twelve Tables.

L. Sextius is elected the first plebeian consul.

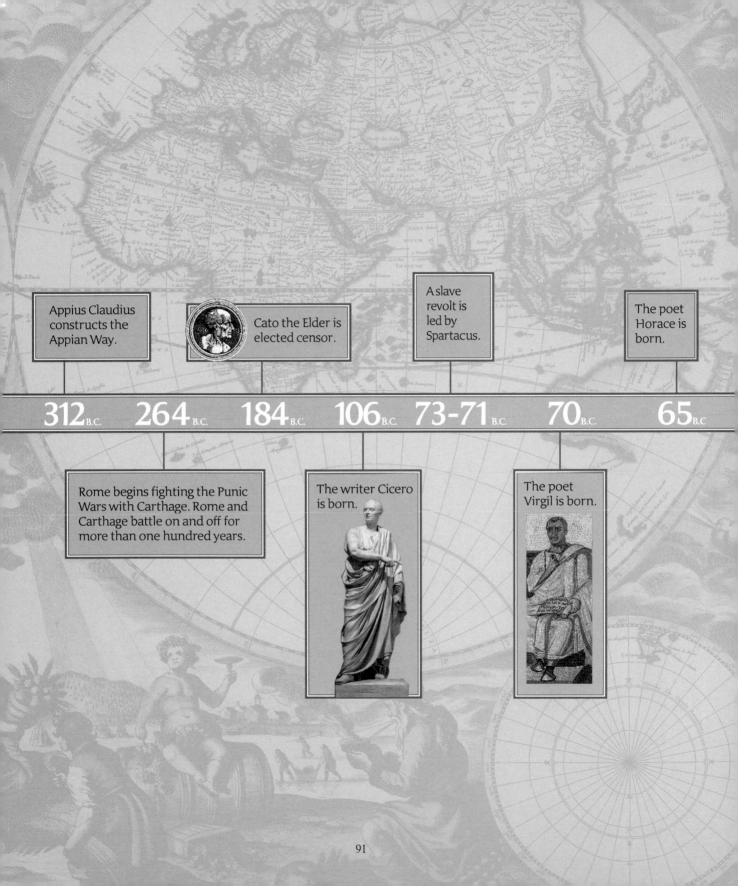

Appius Claudius constructs the Appian Way.

Cato the Elder is elected censor.

A slave revolt is led by Spartacus.

The poet Horace is born.

312 B.C. **264** B.C. **184** B.C. **106** B.C. **73-71** B.C. **70** B.C. **65** B.C.

Rome begins fighting the Punic Wars with Carthage. Rome and Carthage battle on and off for more than one hundred years.

The writer Cicero is born.

The poet Virgil is born.

The Theater of Pompey, which seats about 80,000 people, opens in Rome.

Mark Antony and Cleopatra are defeated by Octavian in the Battle of Actium.

Rome experiences a time of political stability and economic growth known as Pax Romana, or "Roman Peace."

The year of the four emperors: Galba, Vitellius, Otho, and Vespasianus. The writer Suetonius is born.

58-50 B.C.   **55** B.C.   **44** B.C.   **31** B.C.   **4** B.C.   A.D. **27-180**   A.D. **56**   A.D. **69**.

Julius Caesar invades Gaul and defeats the Celtic tribes. He writes a journal called *The Gallic War* about his experiences.

Julius Caesar assumes control of the senate. He is assassinated on the ides of March.

The possible year of the birth of Jesus Christ.

The Roman historian Tacitus is born.

Construction of the Coliseum is completed.

Hadrian orders the Roman army to build a wall in what is now Great Britain, along the northern boundaries of the Roman Empire.

Emperor Constantine founds the new capital of Constantinople.

End of the Roman Empire.

| A.D. 79 | A.D. 81 | A.D. 117-138 | A.D. 122 | A.D. 192-197 | A.D. 330 | A.D. 455 | A.D. 476 |

Pompeii and Herculaneum are destroyed by the eruption of Mount Vesuvius. Pliny the Elder is killed while observing the eruption up close.

Hadrian is emperor.

A series of civil wars in Rome creates unrest.

Rome is occupied by the Vandals.

Marcus Vipsanius Agrippa

56–12 B.C.

Agrippa led armies to many victories for Octavian, who later became Rome's first emperor. Agrippa's most famous victory was at the Battle of Actium, where he defeated Mark Antony and the Egyptian queen Cleopatra. Although Agrippa was never emperor, he was so popular that Roman coins were struck in his name.

Gaius Caesar Augustus Germanicus,
also known as Caligula

A.D. 12–41

Caligula was a kind and friendly Roman leader who eventually became an infamous emperor. His bizarre behavior while emperor, including nominating his horse as consul, convinced the Romans that he was insane. He was finally assassinated by his own bodyguards.

Marcus Porcius Cato,
also known as Cato the Elder

234–149 B.C.

Cato, a wealthy Roman lawyer, believed in the traditional values of Rome. He served as military general, quaestor, aedile, praetor, consul, and censor during his career in Roman government. He wrote a history of Rome, most of which is now lost.

Marcus Tullius Cicero

106–43 B.C.

Cicero was born into a wealthy family and eventually rose to become a lawyer and consul. He was a prolific writer, producing more than fifty speeches, over eight hundred letters, and almost two thousand pages of philosophical writings including his two most famous, *On Duties* and *On the Republic*.

Hypatia

A.D. ?–415

Hypatia was a rare female intellectual and teacher during the later Roman Empire. Her philosophy and scientific lectures were very popular at the University of Alexandria. However, the Christian leaders considered her to be a dangerous pagan and had her clubbed to death in the streets.

Gaius Julius Caesar

100–44 B.C.

Caesar was a military leader who made a name for himself by conquering Gaul, invading Britain, then writing a popular work, *The Gallic Wars*, about his exploits. He appointed himself dictator for life, only to be assassinated by a group of senators jealous and fearful of his power. His life and death were immortalized in the Shakespearean play *Julius Caesar*.

Lucretia

510 B.C.

This honorable lady was the wife of Collatinus, a respected Roman in the court of the Etruscan king Tarquin. Legend says that while her husband was away, Tarquin's son Sextus attacked her. After the attack she stabbed herself rather than endure the shame. Brutus, a friend of Lucretia's husband Collatinus, vowed to avenge her and topple the monarchy. Aided by other leading citizens and the public, they overthrew Tarquin and established the Roman Republic.

Gaius Plinius Secundus,
also known as Pliny the Elder

A.D. 23–79

A natural historian and scientist, Pliny is most remembered for how he died: in the eruption of Vesuvius in A.D. 79 that buried the Roman cities of Pompeii and Herculaneum. Pliny had a love of nature and was one of the first Romans to study natural phenomena from a scientific point of view.

Gaius Plinius Caecilius Secundus,
also known as Pliny the Younger

62 B.C.– A.D. 115

Nephew of Pliny the Elder, Pliny the Younger was a highly respected public servant and nobleman. He served as praetor and consul and was the friend of the emperor Trajan. However, his most lasting contribution is his writings. He published books on poetry and a book of his letters, which became popular reading. He immortalized his uncle's death in the eruption of Vesuvius in his letters.

Lucius Annaeus Seneca,
also known as Seneca the Younger

3–4 B.C.– A.D. 52

Born in the Roman provinces in Spain, Seneca rose through the ranks to become senator. He also tutored and advised the famous Roman emperor Nero. In A.D. 41, he was sent into exile for having an affair with the emperor Caligula's daughter, although historians now doubt the story. He was a playwright specializing in tragedies. His work influenced much of modern European literature.

aedile a government official in charge of taking care of all public buildings and temples and oversaw the food and water supplies and public events

Armilustrum a military festival held in October to honor Mars, the god of war

auctorati people who signed up to be gladiators for a fee

augur priests who were trained to read the will of gods from events, such as the feeding habits of chickens

aqueduct a large bridge built to carry water

cavalry soldiers who fight while riding horses

censor a government official who oversaw construction projects and kept track of how many citizens there were and what property they had

centuries voting units in the comitia centuriata assembly determined by age and wealth

century a group of one hundred (later eighty) soldiers

collegae two magistrates in the same position or office

collegium pontificum the college of priests

colonnade a series of columns

consul a top government official who worked on laws and oversaw the senate

cuirass a type of body armor worn by soldiers

curiae wards or districts

cursus honorum the path a person would follow to have a political career; means "course of honors"

eques gladiator who fought on horseback

essedarii gladiators who used chariots

familia rustica the class of slaves that worked outside of the home, doing such tasks as farming and herding animals

flamen an official appointed to serve the state gods, such as Jupiter and Mars

familia urbana the class of slaves that worked in the home, doing such tasks as cooking and cleaning

forum a marketplace

haruspex a priest who specialized in interpreting the will of the gods through the study of animal entrails

galli gladiators who used heavy weapons in fighting

heredity something passed down from generation to generation

imperium the power to rule

lanistae a person who trained gladiators

legion a collective name for the soldiers in the early Roman army

lorica segmentata body armor worn by soldiers made from metal plates held together by leather straps

magistrate a general term for a government official

maniple a small fighting unit of soldiers

Matronalia the festival held in March to honor the goddess Juno

monstra a strange or bizarre event foretold by priests known as haruspices

paterfamilias the name given a father; means "father of the family"

patrician member of wealthy class

phalanx a formation of soldiers used in battle; soldiers stand side-by-side, forming a wall

philosophy the study of truth, wisdom, and knowledge

plebeian a member of lower classes

pontifex maximus the top religious official or chief priest

praetor one of the most powerful judges in Rome

probatio an interview to enter the military

proconsul a governor of a Roman province

quaestor a financial officer in the government

rex sacrorum a special type of priest who played an important role in religious rituals

sacred vow a person promised to give a god a gift if the god granted his or her request

satirist a writer who ridicules or pokes fun at people, society, or events

servi privati slaves who were owned by individuals

servi publici slaves who were owned by the government and often had difficult or dangerous jobs

stoa a series of columns

Stoicism a system of beliefs that stressed the importance of being virtuous and that everyone and everything in the universe has a purpose

tribune a tribal officer in the early Roman military

Vinalia the Festival of Wine, which honored the god Jupiter, held in August

Books

Amery, Heather. *Rome and Romans.* Newton, MA: EDC Publications, 1998.

Carlson, Laurie. *Classical Kids: An Activity Guide to Life in Ancient Greece and Rome.* Chicago: Chicago Review Press, 1998.

Connolly, Peter. *Ancient Rome.* New York: Oxford University Children's Books, 2001.

Corbishley, Mike. *The Romans.* New York: Peter Bedrick Books, 2001.

James, Simon. *Eyewitness: Ancient Rome.* New York: Penguin Books, 2002.

Nardo, Don. *Rulers of Ancient Rome.* San Diego, CA: Lucent Books, 1999.

Videos

Ancient Rome: Story of an Empire. A&E Home Entertainment, 1998.

Just the Facts: Ancient Rome. Goldhil Home Media, 2001.

Lost Treasures of the Ancient World 1: Ancient Rome. Kultur Video, 1999.

Organizations and Online Sites

Ancient Rome: Images and Pictures
http://clawww.lmu.edu/faculty/fjust/Rome.htm

This site includes more than two hundred clear photographs of many Roman objects, such as sculptures, buildings, and ruins.

The British Museum
Great Russell Street
London WC1B 3DG
http://www.thebritishmuseum.ac.uk/

The British Museum, one of the premier museums in the world, houses thousands of Roman artifacts and sculptures.

Horace's Villa
http://www.humnet.ucla.edu/horaces-villa/Contents.html

This detailed site is dedicated to the archaeological excavation of the villa of the Roman writer Horace.

J. Paul Getty Museum
1200 Getty Center Drive
Los Angeles, CA 90049
http://www.getty.edu/

Visitors to this site can see Roman artwork, sculptures, and other artifacts of Roman life.

Maecenas: Images of Ancient Greece and Rome
http://wings.buffalo.edu/AandL/Maecenas/general_contents.html

This site includes dozens of beautiful images of Roman architecture.

Metropolitan Museum of Art
1000 Fifth Avenue
New York, NY 10028-0198
http://www.metmuseum.org

Many Roman artifacts, including sculpture, mosaics, and textiles, can be seen on this Web site, including a life-size reproduction of a Roman bedroom.

National Archaeological Museum of Naples
Piazza Museo 19
Naples, Italy
http://www.italiansrus.com/articles/namnaples.htm

This Italian museum houses many artifacts from the Roman city of Pompeii.

Odyssey Online
http://www.emory.edu/ODYSSEY
This site contains a wealth of information on several ancient civilizations, including Rome.

The Romans
http://www.bbc.co.uk/schools/romans/
Learn about many aspects of ancient Rome, including buildings, roads, the military, and daily life.

About the Author

Allison Lassieur has written more than fifty books about history, world cultures, ancient civilizations, science, and current events. She lives with her husband in Easton, Pennsylvania.